The
World Class MRO
Event Team

Dramatically Improving the Customer Experience During Product Maintenance, Repair and Overhaul Events

Meet the author

Brent is the President of The Finnamore Group. Since 1993 Brent has helped hundreds of companies in dozens of industries spanning 20 countries to increase their sales revenues through a proprietary blend of consulting, coaching and skills training. Working with the leadership and front-line teams of his clients, Brent customizes his approach to each client to provide optimal results. He has been published in success magazines and business publications throughout North America and has written several books on B2B sales, customer service and performance improvement.

Brent resides in Montreal with his family. In his spare time he is an avid marathon runner and Ironman triathlete.

To contact Brent to speak at your next executive offsite or to learn how his programs can help you achieve your top line growth objectives:

email: brent.finnamore@thefinnamoregroup.com

website: www.thefinnamoregroup.com

blog: http://brentfinnamore.wordpress.com

Introduction

Since I started working with and studying companies in 1993, I would say with confidence that out of the many hundreds of them, every single one saw room to improve their customer satisfaction metrics. I have never once encountered an organization that was completely satisfied with the quality of their service. I would speculate that those who were in fact complacent with their customers probably aren't around today.

While customer satisfaction is not the only metric that matters, it's certainly a central one. For one thing, customer satisfaction levels are a lagging indicator of many different aspects of an organization's health. Organizations also know that high customer satisfaction usually means lower acquisition costs (because of lower customer churn), lower concession costs (because customers are unhappy less often) and higher revenues (because they buy more and your reputation grows).

While a lot has been written about customer service, virtually nothing has been written about MRO organizations and the specific, unique implications for them when seeking to achieve customer service excellence. An MRO organization is one that performs maintenance, repairs and overhauls for products. When most people think of MRO they often think of heavy equipment like aircraft engines. In fact, the products could also be smart phones, helicopter controls, automobiles, laptops or bicycles. The products being maintained, overhauled or repaired may or may not have been sold to the customer by the MRO organization. Perhaps they were bought from another company or perhaps from the OEM (original equipment manufacturer) side of that same large company.

The Event Team is the group of various functions that are involved in the MRO process. Event Teams are typically comprised of a front-line customer-facing function, often called customer support, along with all of the other functions involved in the Event (technicians, mechanics, finance, logistics, engineering, etc.). A world-class Event Team is "spearheaded" but not necessarily led, by the customer support function, since they are the interface with the customer. A great deal of pressure is involved with this responsibility. In PART I we will discover an enormous opportunity to dramatically improve the customer's experience in the MRO enterprise by optimizing the performance of the entire Event Team. In PART II we will learn about the critical role of the Customer Event Manager (CEM) – part of the customer support function and a key member of the Event Team – and how to optimize this customer-facing role to provide world-class service.

The following summary of world-class Event Teams serves as both an introduction to the content of this book and as a starting point to reflect on the degree to which your Event Team measures against it.

1. World-class Event management can only emerge from the full, consistent collaboration of each and every member of the Event Team. No one can do it alone.

2. World-class Event Team members are *constantly* communicating and problem-solving together. They all see this as fundamental to their roles.

3. World-class Event management requires that CEMs be Controllers, not administrators.

Controllers seek to proactively control processes and information flow, not people.

4. World-class CEMs see everything coming. They never wait for bad news – they proactively search for signs of potential variance on every engine visit.

5. World-class Event Teams never automatically accept variance - they work with each other to try to eliminate, reduce or contain any issues.

6. Customers of world-class Event Teams never have to ask for an update.

7. World-class Event Teams always create highly confident options for their customers to choose from (including gates and dates); they never guess. As a result, they are trusted by their customers.

8. World-class CEMs always try to find ways to reassure customers no matter the nature of the update.

PART I

The MRO Event Team

Chapter 1

The King of All Interactions

Let's begin by putting the MROs key activity in perspective. All organizations – MRO or not - operate utilizing one type of management system or another. Regardless of the type of management system used, the most important element of that system is its strategy. Simply put, a strategy is your game plan for delivering sustained value to your owners or shareholders. In order to achieve its strategy, the organization breaks it down into several strategic objectives, which usually have monthly or quarterly goals.

An organization's strategy usually has several components, but the single most important component is the value proposition required to please and retain its targeted customers. Put simply, the value proposition is the promise your organization makes to its customers. On the OEM side of a business, the value proposition is probably high quality, high performance, low cost or some combination of these. On the other hand, on the MRO side of a business the value proposition is about customer service, timeliness of service, ease of doing business, value for money, clear communication, turn around time, and repair workmanship.

This is where the MRO Event becomes critical. When a customer sends their product for maintenance, repair or overhaul, that entire experience is called an Event. Some companies may call it a Visit or a Service, but it all means the same thing. The customer has to hand over their cherished product and place their trust in that company and its people. Events, therefore, are of particular strategic importance because they are more stressful and therefore more memorable to the customer than other types of interactions with the company. Why? Because customers experience a disproportionate amount of worry during an Event. What are the customer's worries? *"Will I get it back on time?" "Will there be surprises?" "Will additional damage be found?" "Will I be blamed for any damage?" "Will warranty be accepted?" "Will there be unexpected costs?" "Will there be long lead times on parts?"* There should be no surprises as you read any of these questions, since we've all had to part with our vehicles, computers or phones from time to time for servicing.

With all of these questions and concerns running through the customer's mind, an Event can be a critical moment in the customer experience, having an unusually strong – even disproportional - impact on their view of the company in general. In fact, *the single most important part of a customer's decision to do business with the company again is how well they feel it performed against the value proposition during the MRO Event.* And why not, their product is being held hostage, after all.

It is for these reasons that we call the MRO Event "The King (or Queen) of All Interactions." Events, and the way the customer is made to feel during their journey as those Events are executed, have more impact on a company's overall strategy than any other interaction. Getting it right is critical to an organization's overall success.

Standard vs. Variance Events

If we wish to examine the elements of Event excellence and the impact on the customer experience, it helps to identify two types of occurrences that typically take place. Most Events will inevitably be either standard or variance Events. Standard MRO Events are those in which Event costs and turnaround times are within normal expected ranges. The product or component is inducted, and the work is completed without incident, on time and on cost estimate target. As long as the value proposition delivered during a standard Event is competitive, the company does well in terms of customer experience and their customers' worries are at a minimum.

A variance MRO Event is any other Event than a standard one. Variance issues are any issues that will potentially alter the standard cost or turnaround time of the MRO process. Drivers of variance include unforeseen parts shortages, unexpected damage, miscommunication between the various functions in the Event team, workmanship or quality errors, customer credit issues, shipping errors, etc. Variance or non-standard Events begin in one of two ways. It may begin as a known variance Event (where the product is sent in with a known problem or symptom) or it may begin as a standard Event and become a variance Event at some point in the MRO process if issues emerge.

When we add the element of variance to the Event,

the impact on the customer experience becomes even more strategically critical. Because of their critical importance to customer experience and the ever-present possibility of variance, it becomes clear that Events require a highly proactive approach by the entire Event team, as opposed to an administrative or reactive approach.

When an Event is managed optimally by a high-functioning team, the Customer feels reassured, satisfied and even delighted. When this happens, the entire company's corporate strategy is supported. For all of these reasons, the Event is indeed *The King of All Interactions*.

The Problem

For all its strategic importance, the Event is at the mercy of a team (the various functions I mentioned earlier) that often doesn't even see itself as a team. This group of people in the MRO organization has up until now perhaps been a group of separate functions, each trying to protect their interests and stay out of each other's way as they support each Event. In fact, they're probably even managed that way. In my experience working with hundreds of companies in dozens of industries across the globe, I have found this to be the case more than 80% of the time. Indicators of such a team include:

- Warring functions.
- Misaligned metrics.
- Frequent miscommunication.
- Insulation from the Customer of some functions.
- "Us and Them" thinking between departments.
- Blaming and finger-pointing when things go wrong.
- Lack of Customer awareness or perspective in some functions.
- Lack of awareness of Customer impact of daily decisions.
- Complacency, apathy and habit.

These problems lead to preventable delays and mistakes (technical and commercial) as well as poorly managed communication with Customers. In other words, variance. As a result, the customer's worries are amplified and their experience with the MRO company is a poor one. This is the last thing a company wants to have happen during such a strategically critical interaction.

If an MRO organization can find a way to improve the overall customer experience during product

Events specifically, the return on investment will be significant. Having worked with many such companies to achieve exactly this goal, I have laid out in this book a path you can follow. Of course, you will always need to adjust the steps in this path to meet the specific needs and circumstances of your own organization.

Chapter 2

Three Approaches to a World Class MRO Customer Experience

I have found that there are at least three basic approaches a company may wish to take in order to improve the customer experience during The King of All Interactions with its customers. Each approach has its advantages and disadvantages.

Approach 1 – Organize all Event team functions under one Vice President, managed with shared metrics.

This is probably the most obvious approach to improving Event Team performance since having shared metrics under one executive tends to drive collaboration. Taking this approach requires a great deal of political will and savvy, as current executives will always want to retain their power and control over their existing functions. This is perhaps understandable since their compensation is tied to the performance of their respective groups.

Depending on the company's product and service breadth, customer segmentation and organizational structure, the employees in its various Event-related functions may perform more types of work than just Event-related work. For example, some mechanics may perform repairs while other mechanics on the same team assemble new components. In such cases, the employees could be organized so that some team members are dedicated only to Event-related work, while others do other types of work within their functions and are not part of the Event Team.

Once you have the Event Team organized under one VP or Director, the shared metrics must be chosen and implemented carefully. Perhaps most importantly, you should strongly consider having different metrics for standard vs. variance Event situations.

Examples of standard Event metrics (where nothing "unusual" is encountered, cost and turnaround time are within expected ranges):
- Percent on-time turnaround.
- Percent customer cost estimate met.

- Percent self-created error- and/or omission-free Events.
- Percent repair/overhaul cost (to the MRO company) targets met.

Examples of variance Event metrics (where non-standard issues emerge, not due to internal errors):
- Total turnaround days beyond standard.
- Total additional cost to customer beyond standard.
- Total cost to the MRO company.

As you can see by comparing these different sets of metrics, without a separate set for variance situations, the Event Team will feel punished for things beyond their control. In extreme cases, this might even encourage them to ignore variance issues and perform sub-standard work during variance Events in order to meet the standard Event metrics. Furthermore, during variance situations, Event Teams need incentives to contain costs and *reduce the number of delay days* as much as possible, or they simply may not care.

The advantage of this approach is that there is less work and risk down the road because well-planned metrics tend to drive the desired behaviors. The disadvantage of this approach is the amount of work and risk needed up front due to required changes to leadership roles and responsibilities, compensation, MRO processes and organizational structure.

While restructuring the Event functions under one manager and with shared metrics can increase performance, I have seen many examples of Event Teams that are organized this way already and yet preventable problems related to communication, foresight and collaboration persist. This is often because of the way individuals within the team functions elect to behave regardless of the structures or processes in which they work. This problem is most often seen during the beginning months of such a structural change. If it is not addressed, it can become deeply embedded in the Event Team culture.

Approach 2 – Facilitate an Event Team Workshop, where you bring the entire Event Team together and teach them to act as one.

What if there was a way to get the entire Event Team to function optimally without reshuffling managers, modifying metrics or restructuring jobs (all good ideas, but as we have seen, involve a great deal of time, resistance and political will)? What if you could leave everything just as it is and still have everyone

– from the shop floor to supply chain to customer support – become more responsive, resourceful, cooperative, responsive and prevention-oriented? In working with my clients to help them meet their MRO customer experience objectives, I have gradually developed a workshop-style intervention that creates a powerful, lasting shift in teamwork and measurably improves cooperation and performance of the entire Event team. When the workshop is designed and delivered according to the guidelines we'll explore at the end of this chapter, the outcomes include:

- A fresh, new perspective on the customer Event experience from the customer's viewpoint, not the company's.
- A clear understanding of each individual's direct contribution to the customer experience during Events. No one is insulated from the customer.
- Definitive proof that the various functions that contribute to the Event are in fact one team – The Event Team.
- Definitive proof that working as one team makes work easier and faster.
- A set of individual actions by every participant to directly improve the customer experience.
- A set of actions by each contributing function to 1) Detect problems before they occur and 2)

> Eliminate, reduce or contain those problems before they reach the customer.
> - A team <u>Collaboration Agreement</u> that binds everyone to better cooperation and smoother operation in all of the key places where more cooperation and support is needed.

When the above objectives are met through the workshop, the following business results are more consistently obtained:

- On-time delivery.
- Improved turn time.
- More flexible, responsive delivery.
- Lower costs (less overtime, lower inventory, less scrap, fewer penalties, fewer free-or-charge services and repairs).
- Improved employee engagement and satisfaction.
- Improved customer satisfaction.
- Increased market share, sales revenues and gross margin.

Research (Feng, Oyunsuren, Tymko, Kim, Soman, Rotman Institute 2019) shows it is possible to nudge individuals to embed new behaviors into their everyday processes – producing higher performance – without changing the processes themselves. Often, it's not necessary to change a process or structure to improve turn times and reduce preventable variance – it is only necessary to change the way individuals elect to behave within that process.

Smooth, predictable, best-in-class Event service requires hundreds of coordinated decisions and actions by multiple departments and functions on a daily basis. Most companies respond to this challenge by investing heavily in the development of robust processes, operating plans and job descriptions. These well-designed behavioral roadmaps are generally accurate, correct and even beautiful. So why do service problems and mistakes persist? Because the people these processes where designed for do not exist - there are no Econs. The economic recession of 2006-7 caused economists to finally realize an enormous oversight; their economic theories unknowingly assumed people would be rational, have well-defined preferences, could accurately predict the future consequences of their actions and are unfazed by emotion. The new Behavioral Economists that emerged at this time such as Nobel Prize winner Richard H. Thaler call these hypothetical people Econs. Not surprisingly, the day-to-day behavior of real people differs significantly from that of Econs. Factors including context, routine, cognitive laziness, procrastination and social pressure play key roles in human decision-making.

In the case of MRO Events, the exact same problem occurs. When performance drops, turn times slow and quality issues increase, management often immediately looks to change the processes, metrics or the organizational structure in order to create greater performance and reduce mistakes and delays. *Optimal results are not achieved because people are still people.*

The Event Team Workshop (ETW) approach uses the psychology of Behavioral Insights to repair the key cognitive errors people unknowingly make as they work in multifunctional teams such as MRO Event Teams.

Cognitive Repair 1: *People believe that they information they have is more useful and correct than the information they lack. If they do not already know it, it is probably not as reliable as what they currently know.* Repair: The ETW employs the discovery process – allowing people to reach their own new conclusions about the customer-impact of some of their routine decisions – thereby making it their idea: Information they have.

Cognitive Repair 2: *People have limited self-control. It takes effort to resist urges and suppress impulses such as putting self-interests first, judging others, resisting others' ideas and refusing requests that lead to more work. This tendency of course interferes with optimal collaboration.* Repair: Certain activities within the ETW increase the desire to anticipate customer pain and cooperate with colleagues to a greater degree to prevent that pain and support positive customer experiences.

Cognitive Repair 3: *People are influenced by their environment. In order to determine right behavior, people often look to those around them. This creates "camps" and "us and them" thinking between functions.* Repair: The ETW resets social norms to new, higher standards by creating moments of subtle peer pressure combined with the creation of new social contracts, endorsed by key influencers.

Cognitive Repair 4: *People resist change, even when they know it is in their best interest.* Repairs: During the ETW participants create If-Then plans. Research shows that when people form If-Then plans it greatly promotes consistency of follow-through actions and sustained behavior change. The ETW also changes peoples' beliefs about their actions. When peoples' beliefs are changed about the impact of their actions (on the customer) as well as the likelihood of success, it dramatically affects behavior change.

When choosing this workshop approach, leaders must ensure the Event Team includes every function whose decisions and behaviors affect the customer experience during Events. These functions include shop/mechanics, engineering, repair development, repair planning, supply chain, delivery assurance, customer support, logistics, customs, spares, quality, credit, testing, etc.

The advantage of this approach is that there is less work and risk up front because organizational processes, structures and metrics are not changed. On the other hand, the disadvantage of this approach is more work and risk down the road in order to maintain the behavioral agreements forged during the Event Team Workshop.

Approach 3 - Do Both.

Of course, engaging in both methods will produce the best possible long-term results. Change the organizational structure to "force" behavior change and conduct an Event Team Workshop to "nudge" behavior change. 1+1=3.

Most of our clients want to use Approach 2 first and do all they can to avoid shaking up the organizational structure and leadership dynamics if they can.

3-Day Event Team Workshop Outline and Details

DAY ONE

1. The burning platform.

In order to set the right tone from the start, a strong, irrefutable argument must be made that action and change is necessary. Some employees and indeed some managers may well be oblivious to the need for change and voice resistance right from the beginning, demanding things be left alone. Alternatively, they may seek to marginalize the situation and redirect everyone's attention to some other problem they feel is more critical. In either case, this can affect the climate of the workshop and seed doubt in others. It can also cause participants to "go through the motions" and not support the new actions after the workshop is concluded.

To be convincing and compelling, the problem

statement must include 1) clear customer feedback that shows dissatisfaction with current Event performance, 2) statistical proof of current performance shortfalls (lateness, mistakes, etc.) and 3) statistics and facts about your competitors that prove you are not currently number one.

All of these data must send a clear and irrefutable message to the participants: Act or die.

2. The King of All Interactions.

Once a discussion about the need for change is concluded and consensus has been built, the Team must understand the critical strategic importance of their jobs. The organization's strategy must be explained and the Event must be connected to that strategy, emphasizing its outsized importance. Participants must fully grasp the many worries and concerns customers have during an MRO Event. The objective is to have everyone in the room understand how critical their individual jobs are to the overall success of the organization.

At some point in the discussion about strategy, the value proposition to your customers – your promises – must be discussed. The group is asked to describe the specific promises the organization makes to its customers. Each one is written down on a flip chart as they share (value for money, on time delivery, quality, transparency and communication, friendly responsive service, etc.). It is emphasized to them that this is your value proposition to your customers. This is how they measure you during Events. Next, the group is asked to rate each promise of the value proposition from 1-10 on how well they feel the customer thinks they are doing. 1 means extremely poor, 10 means extremely well. Each time consensus is reached about the rating of a specific promise in the value proposition, that rating is recorded beside the promise. The ratings from the group are then compared to any customer feedback data you were able to obtain prior to the workshop.

3. Collective force vs. collective cancellation.

Now that the need for action is clear to everyone, it is time to talk about the importance of teamwork and collaboration. Because of variance during Events and the critical strategic importance of keeping our promises to your customers, a collective force is needed.

Collective Cancellation *is the* reduced power *that results when teams think they are independent,* functional metrics *are put above customer experience metrics and teammates find each other's requests and responses suspicious, annoying or inconvenient.*

Collective Force is *the* combined power *that emerges from real trust, real cooperation, a primary focus on the complete satisfaction of each customer, and true teamwork.*

Once a discussion about the power of collective force has been completed, the group is invited to take a silent quiz. Each question is shown one at a time. They are asked to consider each question as a member of their function.

Silent Quiz: Are you currently working in a Collective Cancellation environment?

- Are you constantly questioning the intent and motives of people from other functions?
- Is there "Us and them" thinking?
- Is your primary concern the welfare of your own function and its own metrics?
- Is information treated like currency - guarded, traded, negotiated?
- Is cooperation transactional, and tracked?
- Do people try to hide their own mistakes but point out those of others?
- Is information used against each other, rather than for each other?

- Do people take secret pleasure in the hardships and struggles of others from other functions?
- Do you make other functions' jobs harder than they need to be by blindly driving your own function's metrics?

Of course, these questions are uncomfortable to ponder – and that is the intended effect of this silent quiz.

4. Facilitate two specific teambuilding activities.

The group then attempts to complete two teambuilding activities; each designed to meet specific objectives that support the goals of the Event Team Workshop. The exercises are ideally be done outside for the purposes of fresh air and a change in perspective.

Exercise 1 – Human Knots. The objectives of this exercise are to 1) get people comfortable working together and to begin building trust, and 2) initiate a discussion about the dynamics of cooperation.

Exercise 2 – Turn the Tarps. The objectives of this teambuilding exercise are to 1) give the group the opportunity to work together as one team or work against each other as separate teams, 2) prove that when everyone works together as one team, everything is faster and easier.

5. Map the customer's journey during an Event.

Journey mapping is a powerful to that helps the entire Event Team to take the customer's perspective during an Event and see precisely how their daily decisions and actions impact the customer experience. Chapter 3 details the process of journey mapping, but a brief description is provided here.

Journey maps begin by selecting a key customer and a key type of Event for that customer. Once those decisions have been made, the group imagines being the customer and identifies every step and action the customer has to take throughout the entire Event from start to finish. This is usually enlightening in itself, because the team usually thinks about their processes and their steps, not the customer's.

The next step in the journey mapping process is to cross the various steps of the customer experience with a series of insights that become extremely useful to the team for creating improvements. There is a table in the room for each step of the customer journey (when I facilitate these workshops I usually get the steps down to six, and so there are six tables). People are invited to sit at the table that represents a step they are most heavily involved in. They are also invited to move around to different tables throughout the exercise. Some functions are naturally involved heavily in more than one customer step. At each step of the customer's journey the same questions are explored:

1) What does the customer want to know at this point in their journey with us? What concerns or questions might they have?

2) What are some things that typically can and do go wrong that affect the customer experience?

3) What are the contributing factors that cause each of the things that go wrong?

4) For each contributing factor, how might each Event Team function be contributing?

5) What can each individual in the Event Team do differently?

After each question is explored, the tables share their answers with the entire group and a discussion is facilitated. Changes and modifications are often made at this point. Then the results are posted on the wall under the corresponding customer step. The realizations and insights that emerge from this interactive process are transformational.

By the end of DAY ONE, participants should have completed the third question – what are the contributing factors that cause each thing that goes wrong? – for each step of the customer journey.

DAY TWO

1. Continue and complete the journey mapping process (rows 4 and 5).

When row four has been completed by the group ("for each contributing factor, how might various functions be contributing?"), there will be approximately five sheets of paper on each of the team tables (30 sheets in all) with very precise descriptions how various functions are contributing to problems for the customer (either by what they may be doing that is wrong or by what they may not be doing that they should).

In order to ensure this part of the journey mapping process feels safe to everyone and no one feels pointed at, it is important to first explain the concept of contribution mapping. This too will be described in detail in the next chapter, but following is the basic concept. Whenever something goes wrong for a customer during an Event, it is never one person's fault. That is impossible, since there is always something someone could have also done differently and since everyone's actions are so closely intertwined. To get to the bottom of an issue, it is far more productive to map the various contributions than it is to point fingers and lay blame. Blaming is about looking backwards at people; contribution mapping is about looking forward and behaving differently. Also, contribution is easier and safer to talk about than blame.

2. Facilitate the development of individual actions.

Each individual then walks around the tables and records every single contribution that has been suggested about their function at each of the customer journey steps.

They will have compiled a list of 10-30 issues, which are from the perspective of other teammates. Once everyone is done writing their lists and have had an opportunity to study them carefully, questions may be asked in order for people to seek clarification about any confusing or seemingly incorrect contribution statements. When everyone's questions have been answered to their satisfaction, they create 3-4 actions to address the issues they feel they can impact. The actions must be specific and must be things they will do personally, not actions someone else should take. This point is critical. Once completed, people sit in functional groups and share their commitments with one another.

Standing at the wall where the journey map has been created, the workshop facilitator then asks, "Who has some actions that will improve the customer experience at step 1?" Those who have actions for a given step then share their actions with the entire group. This process is repeated through all the customer steps. This activity will illustrate to the entire Event Team that 1) There are actions to support each step for the customer during their journey, and 2) each individual's actions are critical; the entire Event Team is counting on them.

3. P.A.P.I. Process for best-in-class Event management.

During the last 30-60min of the day, the P.A.P.I. Process is introduced to the group. This process will be described in detail in Chapter 4. PAPI involves four continuous actions by each and every member of the Event Team. 1) Project into the future, looking for red flags and seeing potential variance issues before they even emerge. 2) Act immediately to attempt to eliminate, reduce, or at least contain the variance issue. 3) Prepare a set of options to offer the customer and to communicate to the customer support function. 4) Inform the customer support function and/or any other involved functions immediately.

The group is informed that on day three they will be sitting in functional groups and brainstorming ways to apply the P and the A of the P.A.P.I. Process – Project into the future looking for red flags and Act immediately to eliminate, reduce or contain.

DAY THREE

1. Development of functional P.A.P.I. actions.

Sitting in groups of like-function, the Event Team members are given the following instructions:

a. Make a list of 3-4 things that go wrong in your function, which affect the customer, that you could see coming if you looked a more carefully. Identify only the things you can do something about.

b. For each one, identify new actions to eliminate, reduce or contain:
    -   State *precise* actions and owners
    -   State precise times for *repeat* actions

- State precise owners and deadlines for one-time prevention/improvement actions

The facilitator moves from group to group during this exercise to ensure they instructions are being followed accurately.

Once completed, each function presents their plans of action and discussions are facilitated where the rest of the Event Team can ask questions and make suggestions. Modifications may be made to each function's plans during this process.

The facilitator will retain the flip chart pages containing each function's plans and create a report that captures each function's plan of action. This report is distributed to all attendees of the workshop and to the executive owner(s) of the Event Team.

2. Facilitate a mini-workshop to forge an Event Team Collaboration Agreement.

The Event Team Collaboration Agreement is in fact a combination of five agreements. It will act as the cement that binds the Team together going forward to realize higher degrees of helpfulness, responsiveness and cooperation.

Seated around tables in mixed groups, each table

having a flipchart, the teams answer a series of five questions:

1. Which functions do you believe have a *significant* impact on Events in this company? Answers to this question are used to form Event Team Agreement #1: The Event Team List.

2. Why is collaboration during an Event more valuable than just *the sum of your individual efforts*? What business results can be achieved? Answers to this question are used to form Event Team Agreement #2: The Event Team Purpose.

3. Which specific tasks, specific pieces of work and key meetings will require deeper collaboration in order to achieve those business results? Answers to this question are used to form Event Team Agreement #3: The Tasks and Pieces of Work Where Collaboration Will Be Applied.

4. What must we do differently? What new behaviors will we expect/expect more of from each other as we do these specific tasks/pieces of work? Answers to this question are used to form Event Team Agreement #4: The Collaborative Behaviors We Agree to and Expect From Others.

5. How can we sustain these new behavioral agreements for months and years to come? Answers to this question are used to form Event Team Agreement #5: Our Plan for Sustaining These Behaviors.

The facilitator will retain these agreements and include them in the report to the Event Team members and the executive owner(s).

3. Wrap-up.

The facilitator explains, "Together we have created a new team that did not exist before today. What you do next is up to you. You need to make a decision. No one can make you be more committed to the customer experience. No one can make you improve your contributions to the success of the entire company. These are things that you volunteer to do, of your own free will."

Finally, everyone stands up and is instructed to walk around the room and shake hands with at least five different people, looking them directly in the eye and stating, "I'm in."

Sustainment of new behaviors and actions.

In addition to new insights, attitudes and awareness, the workshop has resulted in three concrete outputs: A set of individual actions, a set of functional actions and a set of Event Team Collaboration Agreements. There are three methods which must be employed to ensure sustainment of these new behaviors:

1. Routine Meetings. The regular cadence of Event-related meetings such as daily production meetings offers both insight into the company culture and a means to shift it. Regular meetings are a breeding ground for both negative and positive habits. During the collaboration agreement phase of the ETW, participants selected key meetings in which they will consistently practice new, optimal behaviors and create their own plans for implementation. Managers must attend these meetings at regular intervals to ensure the new behaviors are being employed.

2. Management Review & Support Meetings. Managers must be given the direct responsibility of holding a monthly structured Event Team dialogue in which employees have a forum to share their perspectives on how well their function and others are doing as a team. Each function may take away one "recommit" – a promise to the Event Team to stay on track with collaborative behaviors and/or to use the P.A.P.I. Process more consistently in

targeted areas.

3. Event Team Teambuilding activities. Fun relaxing events such as potlucks, hay-rides, family gatherings, pizza parties, etc. have a proven psychological impact on the social dynamics of teammates; they reset their neural associations to each other. Moreover, these events are labeled Event Team activities, reinforcing the reality of this new team's existence and pervasion.

Chapter 3

Mapping The Customer's Journey

Journey mapping has now become one of the most popular and effective ways for organizations to visualize, analyze and improve the customer's experience. The journey mapping process is used to understand what the customer goes through during a particular service and to improve the customer experience during that service, ensuring consistency, ease, transparency and seamlessness at all customer steps and touchpoints. Journey mapping is one of the most powerful tools ever invented to drive improvement...if, and only if, real action flows from it.

A fundamental aspect of journey mapping is that it's all about the customer. The processes, policies and systems of the organization creating a journey map are examined, to be sure, but – and this is the critical point - only in the context of impact on customer experience. To companies with an internal focus and a steep history of looking at themselves instead of their customers, journey mapping can be a struggle against ingrained habits.

Done correctly, with a genuine focus on the customer's experience, journey mapping will help an organization:

- Identify pain points and frustrations for the customer so they can be improved – before the customer defects to the competition.
- Improve the speed and ease of service for key customers by removing unnecessary steps and roadblocks.
- Improve communication and ease worry for the customer by identifying key questions and concerns at each step.
- Tell the story of your customer to everyone in your organization so that everyone has a similar view of the customer.
- Clearly connect customer satisfaction to the internal, invisible systems and owners that unknowingly contribute.
- Help ensure your improvement efforts are directed at things the customer cares about, and not waste time and money improving things they don't.

- Bring teams together to resolve specific hurdles and identify paths that will have the biggest impact on customer satisfaction.

Journey mapping can be used to understand and improve the customer experience in a variety of service interactions: Customer onboarding, using a customer portal or other website, MRO Events, on-site repairs, handling complaints, or any other discreet unit of service.

In order to be effective, the journey mapping process requires six things: Executive sponsorship, preparation, the involvement of all contributing functions, skilful facilitation, clear action plans and a sustainment plan for those actions.

1. Executive Sponsorship.

It takes a full day or more for a team or group of teams to map the customer's journey and develop action plans to improve it. This means investing in time away from normal operations, incurring venue costs, investing in a skilled, experienced facilitator that knows your industry well, and creating a sustainment plan to ensure the changes last. For these reasons, executive sponsorship is required.

An executive can be said to be "on board" when he

or she has agreed to fund the initiative, support changes to processes and systems identified during the journey mapping process and agreed to champion the new action/behavioural plans that emerge from the process by following up and holding key managers accountable.

2. Preparation.

We all know the expression GIGO – garbage in, garbage out. If you make guesses about the customer's experience and perception during the journey mapping process, your investment may lead to insights and action plans that are useless. In order to create accurate, meaningful journey maps it is important to have a thorough understanding of your customer. Analyze customer feedback data, study social media, talk to customers to gather insights and anecdotes, and talk to sales and service staff to gather their insights as well.

The second aspect of preparation is to develop the problem statement. Study your customer feedback data, your current success rate vs. your metrics, your competition's performance against your company's, as well as current trends in customer experience for your target customer segments. Ask yourself, "Why should we be trying to improve customer service? What's wrong?" "What needs to change and why?" "What will happen if we don't?" "What will happen if we do?" A strong, convincing problem statement will ensure everyone is fully engaged during the journey mapping process and also increase everyone's commitment to following through with their action plans.

3. Involvement of All Contributing Functions.

To be effective a journey mapping workshop must include every function that can have a significant impact on the customer experience. The key word here is *significant* – whether or not a given function has a significant impact on the customer experience is a judgment call on the part of the organizing team. It is not useful to involve every single function that could ever possibly impact the customer, but it is also a mistake to overlook those functions that do. Nothing is more frustrating to a team than knowing a key contributing function is absent from the journey mapping workshop.

A good practice is to talk with several people in some of the more obvious functions and get their perspective on who should participate.

4. Skilful Facilitation.

A skilled facilitator will be able to optimize the value of the journey mapping event, whereas an inexperienced one will greatly diminish the outcome. An experienced facilitator who knows the industry well will be able to keep participants focused on customers, not themselves. He or she will also keep participants focused on issues they are willing to own and not just complain about, drive for concrete actions with owners and deadlines, manage conflict and steer participants toward "contribution thinking" as opposed to blaming and finger pointing.

After skill and experience, the last criterion for an ideal facilitator is someone outside the company. The fresh perspective of an outsider who is not a part of the company culture will not be limited or restricted in their thinking. As long as they know the industry and have studied the company, they will be able to add extra value with their lack of bias. They will also have more influence and control over the group.

5. Clear Action Plans.

The powerful insights, deepened understanding and appreciation for the customer's experience during their journey with the supplier organization can be transformational. And yet, such insights are of limited value without concrete actions that follow the journey mapping process to create measurable change. In the end, only new actions and new behaviors by every individual and every function will make the investment worthwhile.

There are at least three types of actions that should flow from the journey mapping process: A set of individual actions that are created by each individual for themselves, a set of functional actions that are created by each function, and a set of collaborative actions that are created by the entire group.

6. A Sustainment Plan.

In order to sustain the new actions and behaviors identified in a journey mapping workshop, at least three things need to happen: 1) Behaviors must be linked to key regular meetings where collaboration is critical and decisions are routinely made that affect the customer, 2) monthly follow-up and support meetings must be held and led by key managers, and 3) any process changes must be documented and communicated.

Select A Key Customer and A Specific Journey

The first step in journey mapping is perhaps the most important one – selecting a customer and a specific journey as a template for customer experience improvement. Journey maps are more helpful when they are not watered down and lack specifics. Therefore, using a specific customer who is receiving a specific service works optimally. You can choose a customer based on any criteria you wish: Representing a key segment, most difficult customer to please, significant growth potential, etc. The best choice is a customer who is representative of a larger segment whose experiences you wish to improve.

Once the group has reached consensus on a customer, the next step is to select a specific service. You may wish to choose a type of Event that you service the most frequently (a specific service for a specific product, under specific circumstances), or perhaps an Event that is historically problematic. It also helps create greater impact on the company when the Event and customer chosen has a solid connection to one or more strategic objectives.

Identify the Steps the Customer Must Take Throughout the Journey

During one on my most recent journey mapping events with an aerospace Event Team, we had selected a customer and an Event for our mapping process. I then asked, "What is the first step the customer has to take in order to have their turbo shaft engine repaired?" I received answers like, "First we schedule a slot and once it arrives on our dock, we hold a Gate 0 meeting to plan the overhaul." They went on the explain, "Then we induct the engine…" Like most of my clients, they could not really understand my original question: "What are the steps that the *customer* has to take?" This is very common occurrence for most of my clients – they simply don't have the opportunity to think about the customer's journey in their daily work. They focus all day on their own internal processes and steps.

With some coaching and guiding, they will eventually see what we're looking for and describe the many steps the customer has to take throughout their Event journey. This exercise alone can prove very enlightening. Those steps are then reduced to the six most critical steps and are mapped out on a giant space on a wall.

Customer Steps:

At this point the journey map will look something like this:

EVENT SCENARIO AND CUSTOMER STEPS, NOT OUR STEPS.	STEP 1			STEP N		
1. WHAT DOES THE CUSTOMER WANT TO KNOW? WHAT CONCERNS?						
2. WHAT TENDS TO GO WRONG AT EACH STEP, THAT AFFECTS THE CUSTOMER?	1.1	1.2	1.3	2.1	2.2	2.3
////// Line of Visibility – Customer doesn't see beyond this point //////						
3. WHAT ARE THE CONTRIBUTING FACTORS FOR EACH THING THAT GOES WRONG AT EACH STEP?						
4. HOW DOES EACH FUNCTION CONTRIBUTE TO EACH THING THAT GOES WRONG?						
5. ACTIONS/COMMITMENTS TO DO THINGS DIFFERENTLY/BETTER.						

Participants are asked to sit at a table that represents the customer step they are most involved in. Six steps, six tables. It is a good idea for some participants to move around between two or three tables throughout the process if the nature of their functions means they are involved heavily in more than one customer step.

Question 1 – At each step in the customer's journey, what questions do they have? What

concerns or worries do they have? What do they want to know?

When completed, groups take turns sharing their answers with the entire group and a discussion is facilitated to share thoughts and ask questions for clarification.

The results from thinking about this question carefully and then discussing the various answers as a group serve three important purposes: 1) People whose functions have them removed from the customer develop a heightened awareness of the customers concerns and unanswered questions, 2) those same people develop a better appreciation for why customer support employees are constantly asking for updates from other teammates, and 3) this leads to higher quality and accuracy of information given to customer support in the future so they can better inform the customer at each step.

Question 2 - At each step in the customer's journey, what can and does go wrong that shouldn't and ends up affecting the customer?

This question needs to be carefully explained to the group before proceeding. Sometimes things go wrong, but they never reach the customer because they are corrected in time. Some things happen that the customer may not like, but they're still not things that "shouldn't," such as warranty not applying for some valid reason or the discovery of additional damage. As the step-specific groups create their answers, they should label each answer as x.x. For example, if the step 3 group has four answers, they would label each one 3.1, 3.2, 3.3 and 3.4.

The goal is not creating an exhaustive list of things that can go wrong at each step; rather, to create a list of the top 2-4 things that typically go wrong. The participants are again reminded that the list is only for the specified customer who is journeying through a specific type of Event under specific circumstances.

When completed, groups take turns sharing their answers with the entire group and a discussion is facilitated to share thoughts and ask questions for clarification.

Question 3 – What are some of the biggest contributing factors - which we are willing to own - for each thing that goes wrong?

As with the previous question, this one also requires some explanation. Ownership is critical. A group might write, "Central engineering takes too long to respond with repair approvals." This statement puts the ownership on someone else. No action will come from this statement. Instead the group should write, "Repair engineers at our facility are allowing central engineering to continue taking too long to respond to our requests." Now the ownership is on the people in the room to do something about the problem, rather than just lament and act helpless.

As the step-specific groups create their answers, they should label each answer as x.x.x. For example, the step 3 group in our last example had identified four things that go wrong for the customer. They labelled each one 3.1, 3.2, 3.3 and 3.4. Let's imagine they come up with two contributing factors for 3.1. They would label the two contributing factors 3.1.1 and 3.1.2. Then they would work on 3.2, following the same process.

When completed, groups take turns sharing their answers with the entire group and a discussion is facilitated to share thoughts and ask questions for clarification.

Question 4 – For each contributing factor, how might the various functions be contributing?

This is the most important question so far in the journey mapping process. 5-10 sheets are distributed to each group:

Completing row 4 on the Journey Map

STEP ___

"What (if anything) goes wrong, that impacts the customer?"

Contributing Factor

Contributing factor _____:

"Which functions are contributing to this factor and how?"

Before they begin, they fill in the information on the

top half of the page. They record the step they are working on, the "Thing that goes wrong" and the contributing factor. The facilitator should check in with each group and ensure this is done, along with the appropriate labelling (x.x.x). This is important because later on when a key manager gathers these pages to keep as records, they can get mixed up and it can be nearly impossible to figure out which contributions go with which step. The group is told, "One page for each contributing factor."

STEP 1

What tends to go wrong, that impacts the customer?

1.1 _____

Contributing Factor (one per page):

1.1.1_____

Specific contributions by *specific* functions:

"(<u>function</u>) is contributing by (doing x, not doing Y). (<u>another function</u>) may be contributing by (doing x, not doing Y)..."

Please underline the function so they can clearly see it when they visit your answers later.

It is also important to remind the group not to fill these pages with recommendations on what should be done differently. Ideas have more power if people come up with them on their own. Instead, they are shown a template to follow (pictured above). They are also instructed to underline the specific functions being mentioned on each page so that when it is time for question 5, everyone will easily be able to identify their own function and create individual actions from the sheets.

Question 5 – In light of these contributions, what is each of us willing to do differently?

Once all groups have finished, the sheets are laid out at each corresponding table so that they can easily be read by everyone as they personally visit each table. Participants are instructed to walk around and visit every table, recording every single thing that has been noted about their function's contributions. They must record the customer step, the thing that goes wrong and the contributions by their function as suggested by the sheets.

It should be emphasized that they are to record even the contributions that they do not fully understand or agree with.

Once completed, they will have each compiled a list of between 10-30 issues, which are from the perspective of other teammates. Once everyone is done writing their lists and have had an opportunity to study them carefully, questions may be asked in order for people to seek clarification about any confusing or seemingly incorrect contribution statements. When everyone's questions have been answered to their satisfaction, they create 3-4 actions to address the issues they feel they can impact. The actions must be specific and must be things they will do personally, not actions someone else should take. This point is critical. Once completed, people sit in functional groups and share their commitments with one another.

Standing at the wall where the journey map has been created, the workshop facilitator then asks, "Who has some actions that will improve the customer experience at step 1?" Those who have actions for a given step then share their actions with the entire group. This process is repeated through all the customer steps. This activity will illustrate to the entire Event Team that:

1) There are actions to support each step for the customer during their journey.

2) Each individual's actions are critical; the entire Event Team is counting on them.

Chapter 4

The P.A.P.I. Process for Event Team Members

It is a very powerful achievement to get everyone aligned, involved and focused on improving the customer journey. In chapter 5 we'll build on this new alignment and discover a highly effective method for increasing collaboration between Event Team functions on a daily basis. But before we explore methods to increase collaboration, we must first ensure everyone is functioning optimally in their own functions by being as proactive and responsive as possible for the customer.

When studying Customer service and Event Management Teams, clear patterns emerge among the highest performers. Specifically, four key behaviors stand out. These four behaviors can sometimes look very different in different industries, but the nature of these four behaviors is always the same. On every single product visit the best of the best – *perhaps unknowingly* – follow some version of the following process. They **P**roject into the future, looking for "red flags" and seeing potential issues before they even emerge. They then **A**ct immediately to either eliminate, reduce or contain the issue. Then they **P**repare a set of options for the customer support team to offer the Customer. Finally, they **I**nform the appropriate functions such as customer support immediately so they are aware at all times and can take action.

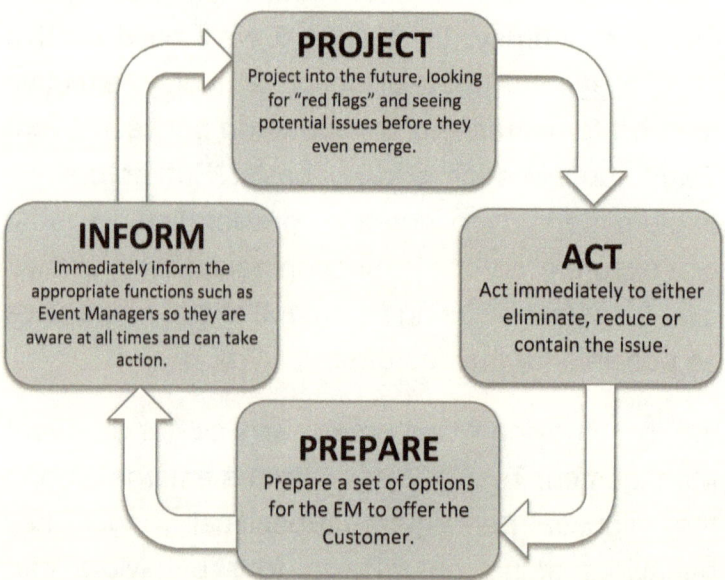

1. PROJECT into the future on all customer

Events, seeing issues before they materialize.

Every single Event Team member, regardless of their function, must be taught to proactively analyze customer data, product historical data, usage data, logistics and customs historical data, reason for Event, equipment performance data, etc. in some cases before the product even arrives at the facility. This activity should continue throughout the MRO process with a handful of frequent issues in mind to look for (cost variance potential, work scope variance potential, turn time variance, etc.). They must also communicate frequently with other Event Team members to stay constantly aware of any emerging issues. If anyone suspects a variance may be imminent, they must talk to customer support and get context on the customer (big picture, important considerations to keep in mind when planning solutions and options) and then ACT with urgency.

2. ACT on any potential variance issues urgently to *eliminate, improve* or *contain*.

Rather than accepting variance issues as cast in stone, Event Team members must instead take immediate action and collaborate with teammates to try and eliminate the problem. If it cannot be eliminated, they must try to improve it or at the very least contain it so it doesn't get worse for the customer.

3. PREPARE options for the customer support team to offer to the Customer.

Working closely with teammates, Event Team members must then prepare highly confident options for the customer to consider whenever possible - customers like being given alternatives. Of course, they must always focus on win-win outcomes.

4. INFORM customer support or other appropriate Event Team functions immediately.

If an Event Team member waits until a regular meeting to inform their colleagues, valuable hours will be wasted that could have been spent taking action. Windows of opportunity may close. Option one is to tell them as soon as it is discovered and develop eliminate-reduce-contain plans along with customer options with their colleagues. Option two is to immediately develop eliminate-reduce-contain actions and develop options first, then inform colleagues.

Now let's compare this set of best practices to those of traditional reactive administrators. It is quite different than those of top performers:

NEWS → ASKED → TELL

1. NEWS.

Average performing MRO employees do not project into the future. Rather, they wait until they experience variance or receive news about a variance and do nothing until that time. By then, the opportunity to eliminate, improve or contain the issue has long since passed and delays and higher costs are unavoidable.

2. ASKED.

Average performers wait until they are asked by customer support before giving an update, or wait until the next production meeting. If customer support never asks, they never receive an update – they just get a big surprise later on when they hear the product is going to be late or the workscope is going to change.

3. TELL.

Only if asked, average performers tell customer

support the bad news, so they can pass it on to the customer.

Since an Event is such an important moment for the customer and presents an opportunity to either showcase your company's exceptional customer care or frustrating lack of care, which process would you rather have working for you if you were the customer? No one likes being kept in the dark while his or her product is being serviced. No one enjoys surprise delays or cost overruns – do you?

Chapter 5

Forging an Event Team Collaboration Agreement

As I mentioned in chapter 3, the Event Team Collaboration Agreement is in fact a combination of five agreements. It will act as the cement that binds the Team together going forward to realize higher degrees of helpfulness, responsiveness and cooperation. When teammates serve each other better, the entire team serves the customer better.

The collaboration agreement works best when it is included in the Event Team Workshop as a final exercise. Seated around tables in mixed groups, each table having a flipchart, the teams answer a series of five connected questions:

1. Which functions do you believe have a *significant* impact on Events in this company? To be effective, each of the Event Team members must feel confident that every involved function is a clear member of the Event Team and that no important functions are being left out. The facilitator should help to ensure the group's answers are complete. Once each group has presented their answers, they are used to form Event Team Agreement #1: The Event Team List.

2. Why is collaboration during an Event more valuable than just *the sum of your individual efforts*? What business results can be achieved? Every team needs a purpose, a why. Having teammates think about what's to gain by increased collaboration is an instinctive motivator. Once each group has presented their answers, they are used to form Event Team Agreement #2: The Event Team Purpose.

3. Which specific tasks, specific pieces of work and key meetings will require deeper collaboration in order to achieve those business results? When teammates agree on exactly when and where collaboration will make a difference, these moments become queues that signal the right behaviors. The facilitator must ensure that key meetings – a bedrock of corporate culture – are also included. Once each group has presented their answers, they are used to form Event Team Agreement #3: The Tasks and Pieces of Work Where Collaboration Will Be Applied.

4. What must we do differently? What new behaviors will we expect/expect more of from each other as we do these specific tasks/pieces of work? Collaboration means different things to different people. Clarifying exactly what collaboration looks like during daily work serves to hone the new behaviors to a laser point. Once each group has presented their answers, they are used to form Event Team Agreement #4: The Collaborative Behaviors We Agree to and Expect From Others.

5. How can we sustain these new behavioral agreements for months and years to come? Sustainment strategies must be created by the Event Team itself, not enforced by managers. It must be their idea. Once each group has presented their answers, they are used to form Event Team Agreement #5: Our Plan for Sustaining These Behaviors.

The facilitator should retain these agreements and include them in the report to the Event Team members and the executive owner(s).

Chapter 6

The Event Team Support Meeting

It is perhaps disturbing to learn that after one year, 51% of post heart attack patients stop taking their prescribed blood pressure medication even though they know it will save their lives (Hill, Miller et al, 2011). Human beings seem to struggle with new behaviors even when they believe the behaviors are the right thing to do – even when their lives depend on it. It follows then that the action plans and collaborative agreements developed in the Event Team Workshop must be reinforced. People need help staying on track. In fact, the blood pressure medication patients who do in fact stay with their medication regimes often do so precisely because they participate in support groups and enjoy family support.

Event Team Support Meetings (ETSs) are regular manager-led meetings to support the continued behavior changes agreed to in the Event Team Workshop. And they are essential.

The Event Team Workshop left participants with three kinds of action plans:

1. Individual actions discovered from the detailed Journey Mapping process.

2. Per-function actions to 1) Detect problems before they occur, and 2) Act to eliminate, reduce or contain those potential problems. These action plans followed the P.A.P.I. Process introduction.

3. Event Team Collaboration Agreement actions – precisely what behaviors they will do and expect from others, and during precisely what jobs, pieces of work, and meetings they will do those behaviors.

Each of these sets of actions must be revisited, reinforced and supported by a regular calendar cadence of ETSs in order to prevent a behavior-drift back to original habits.

ETSs can either be led by the same manager every time or by different managers on a rotational basis. In either case, there are two criteria for choosing an effective manager for ETSs: 1) The manager should be high enough in the organizational structure that they oversee more than one function in the Event Team. If the manager only oversees one function there can be a real or perceived bias that could over time cause the "us-them" gap to reemerge. 2) The manager should be an influential person – one who is known, liked and respected by the majority of the Event Team members.

ETS Meeting Agenda:

1. Set the context for the meeting:

    a. Remind the team of the five takeaways from the Event Team Workshop: 1) The Event is The King of All Interactions. 2) As it turns out, we are one team after all: The Event Team. 3) When something goes wrong, there is always a contribution system involved. 4) Everyone in every function on the Event Team can (and must) use P.A.P.I. 5) Teams function best when they create collaborative Agreements and *everyone follows those agreements every minute of the day.*

    b. Remind the team of the purpose of the meeting – to support continued commitment to the three sets of actions (individual, functional and collaboration).

    c. Remind them that the focus of discussions should always be on things that are within our immediate control.

2. Review recommits from last meeting (begin doing this at the second ETS meeting).

3. General group questions.

    a. *"How is it going since our last meeting?"* You may wish to use a "scale of 1-10," or a "thumbs up, thumbs down, thumbs neutral" device to facilitate the conversation.

    b. Invite people to explain. *"Would anyone care to explain their rating?"*

4. Specific group questions.

    a. *"What challenges make it hard to keep your individual commitments?"*

    b. *"What challenges make it hard to keep your functional PAPI commitments?"*

    c. *"What challenges make it hard to keep your Collaboration Agreement behaviors?"*

    d. *"Can anyone give an example of a positive behavior they experienced from another teammate recently (try to get 2-3 answers)?"*

    e. *"Can anyone give an example of a behavior they have experienced from a teammate that* does not align with our commitments *(give each party a chance to respond/explain)?"*

 f. *"What do you need from your teammates in order to get back on track?"*

 g. *"What do you need from your manager in order to get back on track?"*

5. Recommits.

 a. *"Does anyone want to offer a recommit to the team?"*

PART II

The Customer Event Manager

Are You a Customer Event Manager Without Knowing it?

As usual, Shria was ready. Anticipating the arrival of a customer's aircraft engine later in the afternoon, she was already looking ahead and analyzing the engine's usage data to look for potential issues. As soon as the engine came into the facility for its overhaul she had questions for the production manager. *"When do you estimate the disassembly will be completed?"* *"How will their last flight through volcanic ash affect the engine outcome? What additional work do you anticipate the engine will need?"* Shria didn't like surprises and she learned long ago that the only way to avoid them was to be on top of things right from the start. She wanted every engine visit under her care to be as smooth and painless for her customers as possible.

The production manager said, *"We can probably expect some damage to the compression blades and we'll have to perform a deeper inspection on the cold section. I'd say we're looking at an additional week added to the turnaround time."* Shria knew this particular type of issue could not be eliminated or even mitigated – it was essential to address these problems in order to have a safe, properly functioning engine. Already Shria was thinking about how she would communicate this news to her customer in order to ensure it was well received. She would emphasize the critical nature of the overhaul under these exceptional conditions and explain the damage and its implications for engine safety and performance. Then she would share the go-forward plan, turnaround time and cost projections. Finally, she thought about the options she could offer her customer in case they were displeased with the news. Shria picked up the phone to call her customer who was undoubtedly worrying about the whole situation at this very minute. She didn't know it, but she was a Customer Event Manager – and a good one. Her company did not require her to go this far to take care of her customers – it was simply her nature.

Customer Event Managers (CEMs) are a special breed of customer service professional. Rather than dealing with everyday inquiries and general service issues, CEMs are on-point whenever a customer has to send in a product for maintenance, repair or overhaul.

Most product-related companies unknowingly have an Event-based model within their organizational structure. A customer with a warranty or protection plan for their smart phone will contact a CEM (although the company may not use that title) to have his phone repaired or replaced. When they send in the phone, it is an Event. A customer with a vehicle under a warranty or a protection plan will bring in her vehicle at regular intervals for maintenance or repair; another Event. A customer with an aircraft will ship his engine to the manufacturer at regular time and cycle intervals to have it repaired or overhauled; also an Event. As we discovered in Part I of this book, Events are of particular importance because they are more stressful and therefore more memorable to the customer than other types of interactions. The customer is very worried – *"When will I be able to get my product back? I need it. Will there be unexpected costs or delays? Will warranty be granted? What will be covered by my protection plan and what will not be covered? Will I be blamed for any damage to the product? Will there be parts shortages that lead to delays?"*

With all of these questions and concerns running through the customer's mind, an Event can be a critical moment is the customer experience, having an unusually strong impact on their view of your company in general. In fact, in my experience working with and talking to CEMs and their managers over the years, it is likely safe to say that one Event is worth about ten other service issues in terms of impact on overall customer experience. And why not, you're holding their product hostage, after all.

Customer Events Require More than Administration

Many service professionals who excel in Event situations don't even realize they are CEMs. They are hired for a customer service position and the company does not distinctly recognize the inherent uniqueness of the role. Without a clear understanding of the "Event" nature of product MRO processes, most companies encourage their CEM-like service staff to assume the role of an Administrator. They are trained in company policies and taught to ensure customers follow proper procedures throughout the Event cycle, such as completing forms, proper packaging for shipment, documentation and so on. Of course, this is important. But it is not enough if that company wishes to become known for extraordinary customer service. If a company does not recognize the uniqueness of an Event from the customer's perspective, they may fail to offer distinctive service when it matters most. For these companies, having people like Shria is actually a fortunate accident, rather than an intended consequence.

The Best CEMs are Controllers.

Our research over the past 25 years suggests that the best CEMs are not administrators at all; they are proactive, action-oriented, forward-thinking service experts. They elect to perform their jobs with this style not because their company has recognized the uniqueness of Event management and designed the role intentionally, but because of their personality traits:

- They are outspoken, opinionated, and like to control the interaction with the customer (and with colleagues).

- They are skilled problem solvers.

- They are directive and innovative. They are "take charge" people, driven to deliver fast, easy service and they are comfortable exerting their strong personalities to get things done.

• They are more interested in building and following a clear plan of action than "going with the flow."

• They are confident and vocal.

• While other service professionals offer customers a long list of options, Controllers just offer the one or two they know will best meet the customer's needs.

• Other service professionals try to resolve issues, as you might expect, but Controllers go one step further – they anticipate future issues and make recommendations as well.

• They also tend to shun generic, formal language and communicate in practical, down-to-earth ways.

• They deliver what customers seem to want most during an Event: Clear guidance.

A Guide to PART 2

If you are a director or VP, this section of the book will show you how to design this distinct job function in your organization and how to create the conditions for your new CEMs to excel during customer Events.

If you are a manager, it will show you how to coach and guide your customer service team to be more effective in creating a positive customer experience during Events.

If you are already a CEM (probably without that specific title), this book will show you how others perform this function with distinction so that you may potentially improve your own performance.

Chapter 1 - How the Best CEMs do it: The P.A.P.I. Process For CEMs.

Chapter 2 - Designing and Implementing the CEM Role in Your Organization.

Chapter 3 - Hiring For Talent, Not Skill.

Chapter 4 - Training Your CEMs in the P.A.P.I. Process.

Chapter 5 - Empowering Your CEMs with Authority, Information, Resources and Accountability.

Chapter 1

How the Best CEMs do it: The P.A.P.I. Process For CEMs

Having trained and coached tens of thousands of customer service professionals in dozens of different industries around the globe over the past 25 years, my colleagues and I have had a tremendous opportunity to look for patterns among the highest performers in customer support functions. In our experience, four key behaviors stand out, which are very similar to the best practices of the high-performing Event Teams discussed in Part I of this book. On every single product visit the Best Of The Best in customer service – *perhaps unknowingly* – follow some version of the following 4-step process:

1. Project into the future, seeing issues before they materialize.

2. Act immediately and with urgency when there is a variance or non-standard issue.

3. Position their updates before talking to customers to ensure they are received in the best possible light.

4. Inform customers early and often, so customers don't even have to ask.

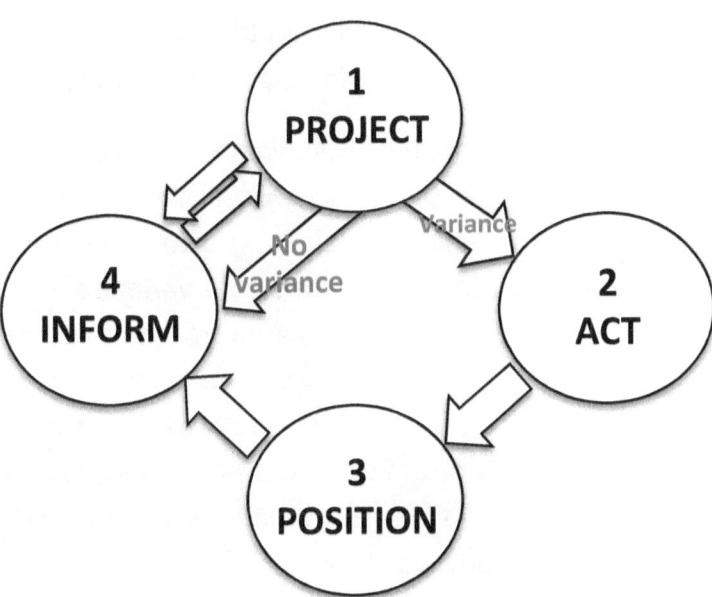

These four behaviors consistently appear among top performers in customer service, regardless of the industry in which they work. You will notice some differences between this customer service version of P.A.P.I and the version we described for Event Team members in Part I of this book. The main differences are attributed to the fact that CEMs are directly customer-facing, whereas the other Event Team members usually are not. Let's look at each one in greater detail.

1. PROJECT into the future on all customer Events, seeing issues before they materialize.

While Administrators focus on what's immediately in front of them most of the time, Controllers spend a lot of time and energy projecting into the future. They don't want to be surprised by a variance; they want to see it coming. Administrators can't see an issue until the repair team informs them and it's right in front of them. By that time, hours or even days have passed where action could have been taken. Controllers spend time proactively analyzing customer data, product historical data, usage data, etc. at gate 0 (initial receipt of product) with a handful of frequent issues in mind to look for (cost variance potential, work scope variance potential, turnaround time variance potential, etc.).

If they suspect a variance may be imminent they get context on the customer (big picture, important considerations to keep in mind when planning solutions and options) and then ACT with urgency.

2. ACT on any variance issues urgently to *eliminate, improve* or *contain*.

Rather than accepting variance issues as unchangeable and cast in stone, Controllers take immediate action and try to eliminate the problem. If they see they cannot eliminate it, they try to improve it or at the very least contain it.

They prepare highly confident options for the customer to consider whenever possible because they know customers like being given alternatives.

Instead of informing their manager and waiting for instructions, Controllers form a position on what to do (absorb costs or charge, offer concessions or not, offer to exchange the product or not, etc.) and make recommendations to their manager.

At all times they focus on win-win outcomes,

considering what's best for both the customer and for their company.

3. POSITION your updates for maximum assurance before communicating.

Despite being highly action-oriented, Controllers take a bit of time to plan their message to their customer before contacting them in order to ensure their update to the customer is well received.

Instead of hoping the *email* won't upset them too much, Controllers picture the *call* going well and they have a plan to ensure it does. They ask themselves, *"How would I like this to go?" "What do I want them to experience?" "What do I want to have happen?" "How can I make sure it goes that way?" "What benefits or extra value can I emphasize?"* If the variance has added value to the product they clarify and dollarize it.

Then they anticipate questions and concerns. They ask themselves, *"What could realistically go wrong?" "How might they react?" "What concerns will they likely have?" "How will I handle it if they do?" "What questions will they likely have?"*

Their preparation gives them confidence when they call. That confidence builds trust with the customer.

4. INFORM your customer early and often, before they have to ask.

Controllers don't deliver "bad" news at all; instead, they deliver updates.

- They call. Promptly. Calling instead of emailing shows their sense of urgency and concern. It also allows them to manage reactions in real time and answer questions immediately.

- They try not to decide for the customer that their news is bad. They frame it as an update and deliver it neutrally – or even positively when appropriate.

- They always try to take some action before contacting the customer. Then they report that action as part of their message to assure the customer.

- They use diplomatic language. They are careful not to use language that makes the customer's pain worse unnecessarily, such as "Denied," or

"Rejected."

- They emphasize value-added where applicable.

- They explain how they have contained or minimized the issue, where applicable.

- They are aware of the temptation to overcommit. Under pressure, it's tempting to overcommit – but doing so will only lead to more severe problems and erosion of trust later.

- They always try to finish their update with a choice of actions/options that come as close as possible to giving the customer what they want.

These behaviors create the opportunity to delight your customers during Events. Customer delight occurs when your service quality exceeds the customer's expectations.

Now let's compare this set of best practices to those of traditional Administrators. It is quite different than those of top performers:

NEWS → ASKED → TELL

1. NEWS.

Administrators wait until they receive news from the

MRO team about a variance and do nothing until that time. By then, the opportunity to eliminate, improve or contain the issue has long since passed and delays and higher costs are unavoidable.

2. ASKED.

They wait until they are asked by the customer before giving an update. If the customer never asks, they never receive an update – they just get a big surprise later on when the product is late or when a bill is sent with additional charges.

3. TELL.

If asked, Administrators tell the customer the bad news. Because they have not taken time to position their message, they often fail to explain the details that led to the variance and they fail to highlight any value added to the product, which would help to justify the additional costs.

These behaviors often lead to customer sacrifice – the opposite of customer delight. Customer sacrifice is the difference between what the customer expects and what they have to settle for in order to do business with you.

It is important to note once again that News-Asked-

Tell is the natural, normal path a customer service professional will default to without clear direction from management, unless they happen to be a "fortunate accident" like Shria in our overview example, and have the personality traits I highlighted earlier (driven, action-oriented, outspoken, confident, problem solvers, take charge, etc.).

Since an Event is such an important moment for the customer and presents an opportunity to either showcase your company's exceptional customer care or frustrating lack of care, which process would you rather have working for you if you were the customer? I don't know anyone who likes being kept in the dark while his or her product is being serviced. I also don't know anyone who enjoys surprise delays or cost overruns – do you?

Chapter 2

Designing and Implementing the CEM Role in Your Organization

Without a specific blueprint that makes the P.A.P.I. process a requirement and clarifies performance expectations, your customer service employees will often default to the News-Asked-Tell path I explained in the previous chapter.

Research by Schonberger, Building A Chain of Customers, 1990, Brown, Breakthrough Customer Service, 1997, Blanding, Customer Service Operations, 1991, and Frei & Morriss, Uncommon Service, 2012, collectively suggest no fewer than 11 steps to properly designing a new customer service role that will succeed and endure.

1. Measure internally to take a snapshot of where you are right now in customer satisfaction, customer turnover, complaints, concession costs and sales revenue.

2. Get buy-in from all key stakeholders in your organization – their support and engagement will be critical to your success.

3. Get buy-in from your affected employees by involving them in the process from day one. Involvement leads to commitment; no involvement, no commitment.

4. Obtain voice of customer data in order to deepen your customer understanding. Survey, interview and visit key customers to find out what they want and how you're doing.

5. Benchmark to establish best practices in other companies, as well as their statistics on satisfaction, turnover, complaints, concessions and revenue.

6. Establish close-gap goals. Decide which gaps you will close and set targets to either improve, meet or exceed industry standards.

7. Dollarize the benefits of closing the gaps and meeting your targets. Build a business case.

8. Working with stakeholders and employees, design the CEM role for your organization.

9. Align your organization's current customer service policies and procedures with the requirements of the new CEM role.

10. Establish pay, reward and recognition plans for employees in the new role.

11. Hire from within before looking outside for people to fill the new roles.

1. Measure Internally.

In order to *start* where you're at, you first have to *know* where you're at. You need a baseline. While most companies measure customer satisfaction and sales revenue, it is surprising how many of those same companies don't measure customer turnover (or it's inverse – customer retention rates), complaint statistics or concession costs. When seeking to change the way in which you do business with your customers, it is essential to measure these things because they have significant financial implications, and you will definitely be improving them with this intervention.

It is estimated that the cost of acquiring a new customer is seven times greater than the cost of retaining the loyalty of an existing one. Adopting a CEM role to your business will have a measurable impact on customer loss. To take a measurement of current **customer turnover** or retention, take all the customers you lose during a time frame, such as a year, and divide it by the total number of customers you had at the beginning of the year. Do not include any new sales from that year.

For example, if your company had 500 customers at the beginning of the year and only 450 customers at the end of the year, its customer churn rate would be:

Customer churn rate = (customers beginning of year - customers end of year) / customers beginning of year. 500-450 = 50. 50/500 = 10%. By extension your customer retention rate = 90%.

If you prefer, you can use this same method on a different time frame such as quarterly or monthly. And remember that you are not including any new sales for the given time frame – which is why the number of customers remaining at the end of the period will almost always be less than the number at the beginning.

To take a measurement of current **Event complaint rates** can be more complicated because many companies do not have a clear, reliable complaint reporting procedure in place, so complaints will not be captured. Yet complaints are one of the most important things to track and measure with regard to customer satisfaction. Repeat complaints are a symptom of a systemic failure on the part of your organization. It is estimated that one complaint represents 20-30 others who did not take the time and effort to complain. *Begin by ensuring you are tracking all Event-related complaints.*

It is important to note that we are specifically focusing the number of complaints in a given time frame that are related to customer Events. There are many aspects of complaints we cold be measuring, average complaint resolution time, percentage of unresolved complaints, percent of increase or decrease in complaints over the past year, number of escalations to management, etc. All we want here is a simple metric – a reliable count of the number of complaints received, in any channel, over the past year, quarter or month, related to a customer Event.

When your organization fails to satisfy a customer – especially a key customer – they may either demand a concession or your managers may elect to offer one. They add up. A CEM-oriented job design will reduce concession costs, and therefore should be tracked. Your finance department will be able to provide you with the data on current **customer Event concession costs**, but first you will need to provide them with parameters. You are looking for the amount of money *or equivalent value* given to a customer to compensate them for their displeasure during an Event. Again, you can organize this data per month, per quarter or per year.

Although most of our clients over the years do in fact measure **customer satisfaction,** we have had a few that don't. At a minimum, you should survey your customers once a year to inquire about their satisfaction with your service. Ideally, a transactional survey should also be given to your customers following each Event.

There are many variables that determine whether or not a satisfied customer will continue to give you their business, but it is a general assumption that happy customers will continue to support revenues. Measuring **sales revenues** is important because when you get better at managing customer Events, it will most definitely have some impact on revenue growth. Satisfied customers will return and word will spread about your service reputation, thereby attracting new customers and making the sales team's job easier. This important data should be captured.

Some companies generate non-sales revenues from investments, so we want to specifically measure sales revenues – the revenues that result from customers choosing to give you their business because they are happy with your service. As with concession costs, your finance department will be able to furnish these numbers.

Once you have these numbers (turnover, complaints, concession costs, satisfaction and revenues) you will not only have a solid baseline against which to measure later, you will also have the beginnings of a compelling problem statement. It will form the foundation of your business case used to get buy-in from your stakeholders and employees.

2. Get Buy-In From Stakeholders.

As you have no doubt experienced personally, there

are many possible degrees of change in an organization. Introducing new documents and tools is a relatively low-level change that creates very little anxiety or disruption for people. Deciding to enter new markets or offer entirely new products is a major change that will impact many, if not all people in your organization. Creating a new CEM role or fine-tuning an existing role is a change that probably lies somewhere in the middle of these two extremes. While you are not turning the company upside-down, you are making significant changes that will affect the lives of many people. Stakeholder buy-in and support will be essential, and now that you have some baseline measures it is time to engage them.

Stakeholders are decision makers who have a vested interest in your proposal. They will be affected by the proposed change and/or their support will be needed. For the Event-related scope we're targeting, the natural stakeholder groups will be the MRO team (you might call them the shop, operations, or the repair techs), the parts/spares team, finance, contracts and possibly logistics (shipping). Because the new CEM role will have more authority than before, the buy-in and cooperation from these groups will be critical. By far the greatest support, however, will need to come from the VPs of both customer service and operations. They are probably the first stakeholders you should talk to.

Your presentation to the stakeholders will have four parts:

1. The Problem:

Customer Events are critical moments where customers form a particularly strong impression about the quality of our service and our organization does not currently have this formal position – CEMs. Without this formal position, service providers default to the News-Asked-Tell path rather than the Project-Act-Position-Inform path. We are therefore missing the opportunity to differentiate in this important area. Our current metrics in satisfaction, revenues, complaints, customer turnover and concessions show room for improvement.

2. The Opportunity:

Differentiate from our competitors by providing best-in-class customer experience around customer Events. This will have a positive impact on all five metrics.

3. The Proposal:

Support the execution of next steps and if feasible,

design and implement the new CEM role in our organization.

4. Next Steps:

1. Get buy-in from employees.

2. Obtain VOC.

3. Benchmark other companies.

4. Establish gap-close goals.

5. Dollarize benefits and complete business case.

6. Design new CEM role.

7. Align policies and procedures.

8. Hire from within first.

9. Establish compensation plan.

10. Develop training program.

3. Get Buy-In From Employees.

Involvement of affected employees should also begin at this time. The earlier they are involved, the more time they have to adapt to the idea and the more opportunity they have to help shape the new role. When people help to develop something new and can see their ideas being incorporated, they have a much greater sense of ownership and commitment.

The most obvious place to start is with the employees who already perform the unofficial CEM role. When you share the presentation with them (essentially the same presentation you shared with the stakeholders) you will undoubtedly hear people say things like, *"I've been saying this for years,"* and *"It's about time someone untied my hands."* You will also meet some resistance due to the fear of change in general and the concern about being given more responsibility.

Always acknowledge concerns. Answer resistance by beginning with some form of agreement with part of what they say. *"That's a good point...so perhaps our objective should be to..."* *"You're right about...and at the same time though..."* *"I agree, we'll have to be very careful to avoid..."* Remember that buy-in is a process, not an event. It's a process of little evens – and it takes time for people to get comfortable with a new way of working. Objections are a normal, natural part of the process of accepting something new. Don't shut them out or ostracize them for having objections.

4. Obtain Voice of Customer (VOC) Data.

With the help of your stakeholders and employees, your next step will be to survey and interview your customers in order to find out what they need the Event process to do for them. *Does it need to be faster? Does it need to provide more transparency? Do they need to be offered more alternatives in the event of variance? Do they want the whole Event experience to be easier, or to have fewer steps?* Your customers will show you the way, if you only ask them.

To obtain VOC, employ both surveys and interviews. Each of these methods compliments the other. With surveys, you can only ask high-level questions but you get a greater volume of responses; with interviews or focus groups, you can ask much deeper questions but to fewer people. Your questions should be designed to inquire about their satisfaction with (using surveys) and their recommendations for (using interviews) four things:

1. Accuracy and timeliness of information.
2. Ease and speed of doing business with you.

3. Choice/options.

4. Consistency.

Research by the Gallup organization who surveyed over a million customers across the globe (M. Buckingham & C. Coffman, <u>First, Break All the Rules,</u> 1999) found that these are the four things all customers want from their suppliers.

5. Benchmark other Companies.

Armed with both current metrics of your organization and VOC on what customers want from you, you now have a framework for comparison to similar companies with which you do not directly compete.

"Benchmarking" is just a complicated word for comparison. The idea is to select other well-performing Event management organizations, ask them to share their metrics and best practices, then use that data as a standard against which to establish gaps or opportunities. The goal, of course, is to manage customer Events better, faster and cheaper.

Without benchmarking how do you know if your current metrics are good enough? You need context. You may discover for example that other companies average 85% customer satisfaction on transactional Events, while your company is at 70%. Now you see the gap and you can choose to target that gap to close.

6. Establish Close-Gap Goals.

As you will no doubt learn from other organizations having benchmarked them, you will have gaps. You will next need to identify gaps and work with your stakeholders to decide which gaps you wish to close. You may elect to close all of them, or you may decide to close some and merely improve others for now. You will be closing those gaps with the design and implementation of your new CEM role, driven by the P.A.P.I. process.

It is important to manage stakeholder expectations at this point. The new CEM role hasn't even been designed yet, and once it is designed and implemented you'll need a lot of time to get people behaving differently and breaking old News-Asked-Tell habits. Even then, it will take months to see the metrics move, depending on the frequency of your Events, your surveying process and the size of your organization. Therefore, your timelines for your goals should be anywhere from 6-12 months after implementation.

7. Dollarize the Benefits. Build a Business Case.

Closing gaps in customer satisfaction, complaints, concession costs, revenues and customer turnover will reap financial payoffs. Your next task is to dollarize those benefits and create a business case that justifies the investment in designing and implementing a CEM role.

Dollarizing increased revenues and reduced concession costs is straightforward, but complaints, satisfaction and turnover are a bit more intangible. While there is no reliable way to dollarize customer satisfaction, you can dollarize complaints and turnover. You'll need to do the same thing that finance professionals do – estimate. Einstein said, "All models are wrong, some are useful."

Calculating Cost of Complaints

_____ Number of complaints (in given timeframe)

_/.08_ Divide by 8%: average number that actually do complain – some estimates are as low as 4%

= _____ Total dissatisfied customers

x _24_ Average dissatisfied customer tells/influences 24 people, who probably won't buy your product. Twenty-four is the common number used by companies, but this is not backed up by citing an actual study.

= _____ Reach

x $_____ Multiply by the price of product

=_____ Total lost revenues

-_____ Subtract the variable cost to produce your product.

=_____ Lost contribution to margin.

As an example, a company with 100 complaints and a product cost of $120 is losing roughly $2 million in lost revenue potential:

____100____ Number of complaints.

____8%____ That actually complain.

____1250____ Total dissatisfied customers.

____24____ Average number of people told.

__30,000__ Reach

__$120__ Product price.

$3,600,000 Lost revenues.

$1,350,000 Variable cost to manufacture.

$2,250,000 Lost contribution to margin.

While this cost model makes some assumptions, it does present enlightening information on the potential cost of complaints and it will get the conversation going with your stakeholders and employees.

Calculating Cost of Customer Turnover

Take your overall cost of acquiring new customers and divide it by the number of new customers in a given time frame. This gives you the cost of acquiring one new customer. Multiply that number by the number of new customers you have to acquire in order to replace the ones you lost in that timeframe. For example:

$500,000 Marketing costs per year.

$150,000 Total cost-of-sale per year.

$100,000 Total incentives per year to acquire customers per year.

= $750,000 Total customer acquisition costs per year.

/ 100 Number of new customers per year.

= $75.00 Cost to acquire one new customer.

x 20 Number of new customers needed to replace lost ones.

= $150,000 Annual cost of customer turnover.

This number does not include the costs associated to setting up the new accounts. It also doesn't include costs associated with trying to retain the customers who left anyway.

Armed with this financial information, you will be ready to prepare your business case to your stakeholder and employee groups in order to finalize their approval and support.

Develop and Present Your Business Case

Your business case will be similar to your original proposal, but with numbers. You have already described the problem in your previous presentation but now you can add compelling financial numbers to reinforce it.

The opportunity portion of your business case will

now identify the VOC data you gathered and also the gaps that you propose to close.

Your next steps will be to Design new CEM role, align policies and procedures, hire from within first, establish the compensation plan and develop training program.

8. Design the CEM Role.

A) Clarify CEM job responsibilities. Following is an example of the key job responsibilities of a CEM. The items in black represent standard procedure when nothing unusual happens, while items in brown represent variance issues, requiring the P.A.P.I. process.

- Contact customer (depending on service agreement) to arrange induction slot for product. Analyze customer data, usage data to anticipate any variance.
- Organize product pick-up (depending on service agreement).
- Obtain customer PO & contract to induct product.
- Chair Gate 0 meeting: Inform MRO team of product arrival, work scope and customer expectations. Share any suspected imminent variance and obtain projections on non-standard

cost and turnaround time.

- If MRO team anticipates non-standard costs or turnaround time, attempt to eliminate, improve or contain the issue. Develop options for customer and inform customer of expected variance.

- Create sales order to induct product. Clear with credit department (depending on service agreement).

- Provide weekly status updates to customer. Plus updates whenever significant new information is obtained.

- Attend MRO team meetings, visit floor re. commercial issues, requests by MRO team for new/used parts approval. Continue to anticipate issues and inform customer.

- Generate/validate cost estimate (depending on service agreement), send to customer for approval. Note any value-added to product.

- Discuss details of cost breakdown with customer if requested. Communicate any value-added.

- If customer negotiates cost or concession, coordinate with management for input/approval.

- If customer wants technical clarification, coordinate with MRO team techs.

- If customer requires on-site visit to review product, coordinate and host visit.

- At completion of product test coordinate draft invoice and final invoice to customer.

- Communicate frequently with cash-before-shipment customers for commitment date, seek support from sales to get payment prior to product shipment.
- Organize product shipment (depending on service agreement).

B) Clarify the Event management process.

Many of our clients over the years have been Fortune 100 companies with deep expertise in designing work processes. We have learned from them that best practice in articulating an Event-related process is to use gates, then map the various job responsibilities to those. Ideally, the gates of the CEMs process should look like the gates of the MRO team:

Gate 0 – receive product.

Gate 1 – disassembly/inspection or product.

Gate 2 – work scope development.

Gate 3 – MRO work completed.

Gate 4 – product testing.

Gate 5 – product shipped to customer.

It makes sense to use these gates because at each gate there can be new developments and new decisions to be made.

C) Create the final job description according to your company's standard procedures.

D) Establish metrics for the position. In addition to the larger per-Event metrics such as complaints, turnover, concessions, etc., you will also require other metrics that by their nature contribute to those larger metrics.

As we discussed in PART 1, you may choose to design these smaller metrics for the CEMs alone, or for the Entire Event Team.

9. Align Policies and Procedures.

Your customer service policies and procedures will need to be scrutinized in order to spot and change any that conflict with the daily execution of the new CEM role. In fact, the policies within each of the Event teams' departments will also have to be scrutinized for such conflicts. As a general rule of thumb, if you find a policy that inhibits any part of the P.A.P.I. process or stands in the way of the behaviors that drive any of the Event metrics, you must change it.

Following are some of the policies and procedures to watch for and potentially modify. This list is by no means complete:

- Reporting relationships.
- Shipping.
- Conflicts between PO and terms of sale.
- Procedures for handling new customers.
- Credit limits.
- Special attention orders.
- Quality complaints.
- Service complaints.
- Returns of material.
- Warranty terms and conditions.
- Unauthorized deductions by customer.
- Allocation of products in short supply.
- Allocation of parts in short supply.
- Change orders and cancellations.
- Customer routing orders.
- Purchase orders.
- Resolving conflicts with purchase orders.

- Pricing.

- Interim price changes.

- Special accounts.

- Discounts and allowances.

- Surcharges.

- Special instructions.

- Credits and adjustments.

- General authority.

- Communications responsibilities.

- Product/service inquiries.

- Order status inquiries.

- Authority for work scope changes.

- Authority for shipping and delivery promises.

- Special orders and variance.

10. Establish Compensation.

Option 1 - Straight Salary.

When considering straight salary with no incentives or performance bonuses, keep in mind CEMs will likely need to be paid more than other service positions due to the increased job responsibilities and accountability that comes with the P.A.P.I. process they will be using. The special skill sets required for this role may not come cheap.

Option 2 - Salary Plus Incentives/Bonuses Linked to Event Metrics.

When considering this option, be very careful to make sure they have enough authority to actually impact the variables that lead to these metrics. It would be disastrous to put people into the new CEM role, train him or her in the P.A.P.I. process, and hold them accountable to the required metrics, only to have them realize they have no control or influence over the variables that affect those metrics.

Option 3 - Team-Based Incentives and Compensation.

As we saw in item 9D – Establish Metrics, you may elect to measure and compensate the entire Event team, rather than just the CEMs themselves. Very often in companies, MRO teams report to a different manager than customer service teams. Silos form and people have no incentive to support each other's objectives. As we work with our clients, the biggest complaint we hear from CEMs is, *"I try to get the production team to give me updates and to consider alternatives to save the customer time and money, but they ignore me. It's just not how they're measured, so they don't care."* Organizing the various Event-related teams into one Event team fixes this problem very quickly.

Event teams can be facility-specific or based on geographical coverage. Team members need to include managers from each of the departments involved with both standard and variance Events (the CEM, the production/operations manager for the MRO facility, the parts manager, the finance manager, the warranty manager, shipping, etc.). In this team-based model, they are all measured and compensated against the same shared metrics. This creates the kind of collaboration needed to deliver outstanding customer service.

11. Hire From Within First.

Few things are more demotivating to your loyal, company-loving employees than to bring in new hired guns for your new role. They justifiably feel slighted and insulted. At the same time, few things are more motivating to your employees than hiring from within. Start there. Then if you have to, you can top off your team with a few people from outside your organization.

Of course, there are pros and cons to both approaches. Hiring from within means people enter the new role with the same old biases and behavioural baggage as before. There will be challenges as you coach and guide them toward new habits. On the other hand, existing employees know your policies and procedures, understand how to work within the corporate culture and have established networks they can leverage to get things done.

Hiring from the outside can mean fresh new attitudes and behaviors, unconstrained by the prison of old habits. This can set an example that inspires others to change. On the other hand, they lack the networks and relationships needed to be productive, so they will likely have a longer ramp-up time.

Chapter 3

Hiring for Talent, Not Skill

"After years of wasted time and money we finally realized - you can't train people to be friendly. You have to hire friendly people and then train them to be skilled at the job."

- Walt Disney

Talent involves the candidate's personality traits. It is the things about them that they couldn't change even if they wanted to, applied to the right role. They are his or her unrelenting nature. Friendliness, for example, is not a teachable skill - it is a talent. Our personality traits determine the things we naturally strive for in our work and life – our talents. Just how useful the candidate's talent is to your organization is also a function of his or her skills and knowledge, both of which are learnable.

There are four classic traits that together form the candidate's personality. Originally developed by Galton in 1884, they are today the gold standard upon which all other personality instruments have been built, and together they form the only trait structure that has achieved widespread consensus among experts. Its prediction reliability coefficient is an incredible 0.8-0.9 – the highest in the industry. It also has multi-cultural, gender-neutral applicability.

Introverted----------------Extraverted

This scale refers to the candidate's *social interaction style.*

Introverts are good listeners, indirect communicators and they get energy being alone thinking and reflecting. Introverts can concentrate for long periods of time and do not crave the limelight. In fact, their alone time recharges their batteries. Their key strengths are planning and strategizing. They are also very good at asking questions and getting customers to talk and share their business needs and their personal concerns.

Extraverts are outspoken and direct. They get

energy from communicating with others and they enjoy the spotlight. Extraverts are persuasive and even forceful communicators. Their key strengths are networking, relationship building and asserting their wants and needs with conviction.

The best CEMs are Extraverts, or at least something in between.

Spontaneous--------------Deliberate

This scale refers to the candidate's *self-management style*.

Spontaneous people are easy-going, informal freewheeling types who feel constrained by rigid processes and who like to make it up as they go along. They have a relaxed work ethic and are generally not well organized.

Deliberate people are disciplined, goal-oriented, productive and methodical. They prefer to follow a process. They are excellent planners and are dutiful and reliable. They have an ambitious work ethic and a high degree of organization.

The best CEMs are Deliberate.

Uncompromising------Accommodating

This scale refers to the candidate's *negotiating style*.

Uncompromising people are steadfast and are not overly concerned about ruffling feathers. They are guarded and do not hesitate to disagree with people who do not share their convictions. They are relentless negotiators who don't stop until they get what they want. They also employ a host of effective strategies in order to get the best deal or action plan possible.

Accommodating people are friendly, cooperative and strive to get along with others. They are highly empathetic and also accommodating. They are likeable and are ready to compromise in the face of resistance from others.

The best CEMs are not too high on the Uncompromising side, but somewhere in between the two.

Fixed----------------------Open

This scale refers to the candidate's *intellectual style*.

Fixed people have firm, fixed views and are oriented toward preserving traditional values. They are conventional and practical. They follow rules and are cautious of new, unproven ideas. They are resistant to change.

Open people are creative and intellectually curious. They dislike routine. They are imaginative and drawn to new and unconventional ideas and methods. They like to think abstractly and innovate solutions for customers. They readily embrace new technology and data applications.

The best CEMs are Open.

Extraverted + Deliberate + Open = Controller.

Controllers are, according to research, the best type of Customer Event Manager (CEM) possible. In escalated situations, they innovate solutions on the spot and actively see them through to the last detail. They build and maintain collaborative networks. They pay no attention to borders and boundaries when solving non-routine problems; they just go wherever they need to, and they don't stop until they get what they need.

Research supports the assertion that talent – something that cannot be taught – is more important to performance than knowledge or skills. But don't be discouraged if you think some of your existing customer service candidates may lack some of these talents. People can make *small* adjustments to their traits - and often those small adjustments are enough.

Research by Matthew Dixon, Lara Ponomareff, Scott Turner and Rick DeLisi (2016). Cited in HBR (2017) Customers Want Results – Not Sympathy provides a helpful guide by categorizing customer service representatives into several types. The top four of those types are listed below - in order of effectiveness:

Controllers (15%) They rank number one in making customer service solutions fast and painless. They are by far the most effective service reps, yet they only constitute 15% of frontline service teams. We have already described their characteristics.

Rocks (12%) They rank second in satisfying customers. They are called Rocks because they are unflappable and optimistic, they don't take difficult conversations personally. Staying calm enables them to be more resourceful and helpful. Of course, customers always appreciate a cool head.

Accommodators (11%) They rank third. They meet people halfway, involve others in decision making and eagerly offer discounts and refunds. Naturally, customers appreciate being given concessions and considerations for their trouble.

Empathizers (32%) In fourth place are Empathizers. They are the most common type found in front lines (32% of front liners). While not the best problem solvers, they do enjoy solving peoples' problems. They seek to understand others and they show a great deal of empathy.

In their research, Dixon, Ponomareff, Turner and DeLisi further explain: The problem is that companies are generally poor at hiring and cultivating Controllers. Furthermore, companies falsely believe the best service providers are strong in empathy, regardless of other traits. Only 2% of managers surveyed said they would hire Controllers, instead preferring Empathizers. Yet research shows Controllers outperform all the other types on a host of quality and performance measures – most notably, reducing the effort required of customers. Clearly, companies do not understand Controllers.

Managers (wisely) looking to shift to a Controller approach in their Event teams face three very important challenges: Hiring more Controllers, teaching other types to be more controlling and creating a Controller-friendly culture.

Hiring Controllers.

The Job Posting: Contrary to intuition, Controllers are not more difficult to find. The problem is the wording in most job postings – it repels them. Generic wording that makes a job look routine, predictable and boring or that signals conformity is a red flag for Controllers.

"Work with existing processes to deliver service excellence," "Meet quality and service standards," "Work with multiple systems, operational tools and processes..."

By rewriting postings, companies can strongly influence who they attract:

"Serve as the customer's primary point of contact and own customer issues from start to finish," "Keen problem solvers who can think on their feet," "Self-starters who are comfortable taking initiative," "Sometimes you won't know the right answer. You'll need to rely on your resources and quickly research a response – sometimes you'll have to wing it."

The Interview: The right posting will attract Controllers, but they still might not make it through the hiring process. Again, many managers have a strong preference for Empathizers and a bias against Controllers. Daniel Kahneman wrote in his 2011 best-seller, Thinking, Fast and Slow, that the best way to overcome imperfect biases during interviews is to design the right questions and hire according to the answers, regardless of gut feelings.

"Tell me about a time when you realized that a process you've been asked to follow a process that didn't make sense. What did you do?" "Describe a time when you needed someone to do something right away, but you knew that person is usually passive. What did you do?"

Training Other Types.

Even with more Controllers in CEM roles, companies

will still have of other types of CEMs as well. So, in addition to better hiring, companies need to consider new approaches to talent development and performance management to help non-Controllers act more like Controllers. The key to making it work, however, is the clear, firm, consistent support of top management to ensure coaching takes place and the corporate culture shifts to support the new behaviors.

Chapter 4

Training Your CEMs in the P.A.P.I. Process

Train The Process

There are at least seven important things we like to remind our clients to consider when we are asked to train people in the PAPI process. We will describe each of those seven points here in case you are considering delivering the training internally.

1. Timing of Training.

The training will always be more effective once participants have had a few weeks or months on the job working in the new role. The experience they gain and the challenges they face while actually performing the job will make them better learners. They will be able to fully relate to the tools and skills taught in the training and they will be eager to learn them. They will also have higher quality questions and make more valuable contributions during the training classes.

2. Outsource or DIY?

If you or someone you know in your organization is both comfortable and experienced in delivering training on interpersonal skills you can DIY (do it yourself). Otherwise, training as important as this should probably be outsourced to a professional training company with experience in your industry and experience in delivering interpersonal skills training.

If you do decide to outsource* the training delivery, be sure to provide the training company with the job description of the CEM role, the P.A.P.I. process and the metrics that CEMs will need to perform against.

* The training company will need to obtain written permission from The Finnamore Group Inc. in the form of a Limited Use License in order to deliver P.A.P.I. training.

3. Training Schedule.

The training can be equally effective when organized into modules or delivered all at once. Employee work scheduling and availability to customers may be factors that support one choice or the other.

If you choose the modular approach, develop four 2-hr modules – one for each P.A.P.I. step. Try to keep the interval between modules to one week or less.

If you elect to have the process taught all at once, schedule one full day of training that covers all four P.A.P.I. steps.

4. Prework.

Approximately two weeks before attending the training, ask participants to think about a) Event situations they find to be the most challenging. b) What they hope to learn in the training. Have them submit this feedback to you no later than one week before the training in order to give you time to incorporate it into the curriculum.

5. Structuring the Training.

1. Introduction to the module or day (schedule, learning objectives, importance of the objectives to their daily jobs).

2. Briefly introduce the entire P.A.P.I. process. Compare it to the News-Asked-Tell model and

seek feedback from the group about the benefits of using P.A.P.I. vs. N.A.T.

3. Explore each of the four parts of the P.A.P.I. process in the order in which they are used. If you are taking a modular approach, you will be teaching only one per module.

6. Case Studies.

Use feedback from the prework from participants about which types of Event situations they find the most challenging to develop 2-3 case studies for applying the P.A.P.I. process.

If you are using the modular delivery approach, ensure your case studies only involve the material you have taught them to date. This is not an issue when using the one-day option.

7. Role-Plays.

Develop role-plays for handling customers and for handling colleagues during Event situations. Role-plays are best used to simulate the critical conversations that need to take place with customers and colleagues at various points throughout the P.A.P.I. process.

Role-plays should be brief – only lasting 3-5 minutes per role-play.

Course Content

The following section details the actual content with should be taught in the training class or classes.

1. What is a Customer Event?

A Customer Event (or Event for short) is the entire process of arranging, inducting, servicing (maintaining, repairing or overhauling) and shipping a customer's product back to them. Events begin the moment you see that the product is due for MRO or the customer contacts you with a problem. The Event ends once the product has been shipped back to the customer, follow-up has been completed and the customer has been given the opportunity to complete an Event satisfaction survey.

2. Standard vs. Variance Events.

Standard Events are those in which you have a contract for regular M/O at regular time periods or usage intervals. As part of your daily job you track each of your customers, contacting them once their period or interval is imminent. The product is inducted and the work is completed without incident. Event costs and turnaround times are within normal expected ranges.

A variance Event is any other Event than a standard Event. Variance or non-standard Events begin in one of two ways. The customer may contact you with a product-related problem that requires it to be sent to our MRO facility. Alternatively, the Event may begin as a standard Event and become a variance Event at some point in the MRO process if variance issues emerge.

Variance issues are any issues that will potentially alter the cost or turnaround time of the MRO process. Common variance issues include:

- Unforeseen damage.
- Unusual wear and tear.
- Parts shortages.
- Supplier problems.
- Shipping or customs issues (logistics).
- Data errors leading to delays.
- Various errors made in the MRO process

(disassembly, inspection, work scope, testing, etc.).

3. Two Approaches to Managing Events.

There are two types of approaches CEMs may unknowingly use as they manage Events in general. The N.A.T. process: News-Asked-Tell, or the P.A.P.I. process: Project-Act-Position-Inform.

The N.A.T. process is inferior and should not be used. It is described here in order to create awareness of potential poor choices in managing Events.

1. NEWS. Wait until you receive news from the MRO team about a variance and do nothing until that time. By then, the opportunity to eliminate, improve or contain the issue has long since passed and delays and higher costs are unavoidable.

2. ASKED. If there is in fact a variance, do nothing and wait until you are asked by the customer before giving an update. If the customer never asks, they never receive an update – they just get a big surprise later on when the product is late or when a bill is sent with additional charges.

3. TELL. If the customer does in fact ask, tell the

customer the bad news. Because you have not taken time to position your message, you will often fail to explain the details that led to the variance and you will often fail to highlight any value added to the product, which would help to justify the additional costs.

The N.A.T. process of Event management often leads to customer sacrifice – the opposite of customer delight. Customer sacrifice is the difference between what the customer expects and what they have to settle for in order to do business with you.

Since an Event is such an important moment for the customer and presents an opportunity to either showcase your company's exceptional customer care or frustrating lack of care, it should be easy to see how this approach is unacceptable.

The P.A.P.I. process is far superior and is <u>required to be used by CEMs at all times</u>.

1. PROJECT into the future on all customer Events, seeing issues before they materialize.

2. ACT on any variance issues urgently to *eliminate, improve* or *contain*.

3. POSITION your updates for maximum assurance before communicating.

4. INFORM your customer early and often, before they have to ask.

4. The P.A.P.I. Process in Detail.

The P.A.P.I. process is used to manage all Events – whether standard or variance. In fact, you don't always know an Event will have variance until the customer's product is received and inspected.

1. PROJECT into the future on all customer Events, seeing issues before they materialize.

- Projecting into the future to look for potential variance before it happens should begin several days before the product even arrives.

- Each and every time a customer sends their product to you in order to be maintained, repaired or overhauled, spend time and energy projecting into the future. You don't want to ever be surprised by a variance; you want to see it coming.

- If you wait and do nothing until the repair team informs you there's an issue, you're already behind. Hours or even days have passed where action could have been taken.

- Proactively obtain and analyze customer data. Does the customer belong to a key customer segment? Do they have a history of loyalty? Is there anything about the customer that suggests an unusual degree of influence? Are they a high-value customer? What, if any, additional protection has been purchased by this customer?

- Proactively obtain and analyze product historical data. Does this product or product model have a history of issues? Are there any "lessons learned" or red flags to consider regarding this product? What are the standard warranty terms and conditions for this product?

- Proactively obtain and analyze product usage data. If you automatically receive usage data from an e-monitoring service check it for any possible areas of concern (performance issues, abnormal usage, proper maintenance, etc.). If you do not automatically receive usage data contact the customer and ask questions. *"In order to help ensure the work goes as smoothly and predictably as possible, can I ask about...?"* Inquire about anything that seems to be missing or unclear (accidental damage, abnormally high usage, insurance issues, next scheduled use, upgrade opportunities, product exchange, credit details, cash before shipping, etc.).

- In cases where you were unable to obtain advance information, meet with production/ operations manager at initial receipt of product with a handful of frequent issues in mind to look for (cost variance potential, work scope variance potential, turnaround time variance potential, etc.). Repeat this same process at product disassembly/inspection.

- If you suspect a variance may be imminent get additional context on the customer before taking action, as this may affect the options you will want to offer.

  o Who is the customer? If a corporation, who owns them?

  o Where are they located?

  o What are their immediate concerns?

  o What customer segment or tier do they

belong to? Are they on a special care program?

o What is the nature of the event? Do we have clarity on liability? What does each scenario suggest as a path? Ex. Likely our fault (we will probably pay). Ex. Likely customer's fault (they will pay).

o What's their overall mood with us from recent history of our product performance and service excellence?

o Are we engaged in any sales campaigns with this customer at present?

o What significant financial issues exist?

o What can we do for them that they have asked for? How flexible and accommodating should we be?

o What can we offer them that they *haven't* asked for?

- In light of this context, develop and communicate your recommendation to management.

2. ACT on any variance issues urgently to *eliminate, improve* or *contain*.

- Work with the production/operations manager (on technical issues) and the finance manager (on commercial issues) to try to eliminate the problem (product exchange, new parts, fast-tracking, extend credit, absorb costs, etc.).

- If the problem cannot be eliminated try to improve it or at the very least contain it so it does not become worse (stop conditions, minimum requirements, etc.).

- Prepare highly confident options for the customer to consider if possible. In order to ensure the options you develop are as reliable as possible, establish gates and dates with the manager or team member.

  o *"What else can we offer our customer?"*

  o *"What is your confidence level in that option?"*

  o *"What is your first critical step in making this happen, where things could change? Let's set a check-in time for that gate."*

o *"What is our plan B if issues emerge?"*

- At all times focus on win-win outcomes, considering what's best for both the customer and for your company. Be cautious not to over-rely on discounts and concessions.

3. POSITION your updates for maximum assurance before communicating.

- Despite the urgency, take time to plan your message to the customer before contacting them in order to ensure your update to the customer is well received.

- Call, do not email.

- Picture the *call* going well and have a plan to ensure it does. They ask yourself, *"How would I like this to go?" "What do I want them to experience?" "What do I want to have happen?" "How can I make sure it goes that way?" "What benefits or extra value can I emphasize?"* If the variance solution has added value to the product, clarify and dollarize it.

- Anticipate questions and concerns. Ask yourself, *"What could realistically go wrong?" "How might they react?" "What concerns will they likely have?" "How will I handle it if they do?" "What questions will they likely have?"*

- This preparation will give you confidence when you call. That confidence builds trust with the customer.

4. INFORM your customer early and often, before they have to ask.

- Call promptly. Calling instead of emailing shows your sense of urgency and concern. It also allows you to manage reactions in real time and answer questions immediately.

- Try not to decide for the customer that your news is bad. Frame it as an update and deliver it neutrally – or even positively when appropriate.

- Always try to take some action before contacting the customer. Then report that action as part of your message to assure the customer.

- Use diplomatic language. Be careful not to use language that makes the customer's pain worse unnecessarily, such as "Denied," or "Rejected."

- Emphasize value-added where applicable.

- Explain how they have contained or minimized the issue, where applicable.

- They are aware of the temptation to overcommit. Under pressure, it's tempting to overcommit – but doing so will only lead to more severe problems and erosion of trust later.

- They always try to finish their update with a choice of actions/options that come as close as possible to giving the customer what they want.

These behaviors create the opportunity to delight your customers during Events. Customer delight occurs when your service quality exceeds the customer's expectations.

Once again, note the differences between CEMs who follow the P.A.P.I. process and those that follow the N.A.T. process:

- Handle things as they come vs. See it coming and control it.

- Short-sighted view vs. Future view.

- Being passive, taking no for an answer from

colleagues vs. Being assertive and pushing to get what you want for your customers.

- Working within safe boundaries and established norms vs. Ignoring boundaries and doing whatever it takes to get things done.

- Responding to customers' requests for updates vs. Updating customers before they ask.

- Relying heavily on emails vs. Relying on phone and face-to-face for greater influence.

Train The Metrics

Show them the metrics they will be measured against for both Standard Event Situations and Variance Event Situations. Lead a discussion about each one and clearly explain its purpose.

Facilitate a group exercise to link the tools and skills from the P.A.P.I. process to each of the metrics. *"Which tools and skills from PAPI will support the achievement of this metric?"*

Ensuring Training Transfer

You already know as a manager that the benefits of training always depend on training transfer. The benefits of training are often hindered by the failure of trainees to use, or transfer, their newly learned skills on the job. Without transfer, the time, cost, and effort that went into the training program are essentially squandered. Training transfer is thus often considered the most crucial aspect of the entire training process.

Manager support and training transfer.

Given the established importance of training transfer, a great deal of research has emerged examining the factors that enhance or inhibit it – and this is where managers stand out. Of the many factors analyzed in this area, supervisor support of subordinates' use of training emerged as one of the most, if not the most, influential factors for ensuring transfer. As a manager, you may be the deciding factor in whether new learning is used back on the job.

Action steps you can take to support successful transfer of P.A.P.I. training.

Fortunately, the best strategies for support also happen to be quick and easy. The goal of these strategies is to create a supportive environment in which trainees do not feel at risk trying the new training. If they feel that you will approve of them continually learning and applying new skills, they will try harder. They will, on the other hand, avoid it if they feel they will be punished in any way, either by customers, colleagues or a manager from any level of the organization.

The strategies included here are broken down into two sections: what you can do before training, and what you can do over time after training. By using these strategies at both stages, you'll reap the benefits that come with employees being motivated during and after training.

Before training:

1. Discuss the upcoming training and its purpose with employees. Emphasize that you believe the training is worthwhile. This can be done as simply as mentioning the training to an employee when running

across him or her in the hall and asking for their thoughts and expectations. It shows that you're aware of what they are learning. Further, by starting a conversation about it and asking for their input, they will need to start focusing on the training themselves.

2. Communicate an expectation that the training will be used on the job. Once employees feel that you acknowledge and value the training, you can also set the expectation that they will need to use what they learn once they return to the job. With a clear understanding of this, your subordinates will be motivated to absorb and retain the information covered during training.

3. Discuss transfer plans and goals. Setting specific goals has long been found to help individuals accomplish their objectives, and this has also been found in the case of training transfer. It is important to note that involving an employee in the goal-setting process, rather than simply assigning a goal, ensures greater buy-in. To do this, start by asking

your employee how he or she will generally incorporate the new learning to the job. You can then expand the conversation to discuss specific situations in which they can use the training. Through this collaborative goal setting, you can clearly demonstrate your support for the trainee and their newly learned skills.

After training:

4. Give employees the opportunity to perform their new skills and to make decisions based on training. This is one of the most critical strategies in ensuring transfer in your employees. Surprisingly, many supervisors overlook this vital aspect of training transfer. In addition to providing opportunities to practice new skills, give your employees opportunities to make decisions based on their training. For example, rather than telling them exactly how to use the training, provide them with a task and observe the decisions they make as it relates to their new skills.

5. Observe the new skills and offer feedback. Once you have provided opportunities to employees to use their new skills, you can observe them and offer feedback. Again, the core principle underlying this approach is to be supportive, rather than critical. Instead of providing only negative feedback and criticizing the employee when he or she doesn't use the training effectively, discuss what they could work on or develop to become truly effective.

6. Reward, reinforce or compensate the use of training. Rebuking an employee for attempting to use new skills just once is enough for him or her to never try it again. In fact, research has shown that just seeing another person get reprimanded is just as detrimental to using new skills as experiencing the reprimand oneself. Instead, focus on rewards. Positive reinforcement for a behavior encourages people (consciously or unconsciously) to want to continue or repeat that behavior. If your employee uses new skills, be sure to recognize him or her and provide praise. A simple and quick "nice work" can go a long way.

7. Use the training skills, ideas, and terminology yourself. Managers can enhance training transfer by demonstrating the learning themselves. Using the skills, ideas, and phraseology from the training demonstrates clearly that you value the training and actively seek opportunities to apply it. This strategy can be as straight forward as mentioning an aspect of the training or inserting a core value from the training when discussing a new project.

Following is a summary of the core supportive behaviors - the PROUD formula. These behaviors have been found to be the most effective, making this a productive place to begin.

- **P**ractice: Create opportunities for employees to Practice new skills

- **R**einforce: Reinforce employees' use of trained skills

- **O**bserve: Observe and provide feedback on skill use

- **U**se: Use skills, ideas, and terminology from training yourself

- **D**ecide: Allow trainees to make Decisions based on newly learned skills

Additional Strategies to Ensure Training Transfer:

1. Commit to a minimum of three years of campaigning: *"P.A.P.I. is how we do our work around here"* messages.

2. Every Event-related manager should create a personal story/platform for why use P.A.P.I. This message should be repeatedly shared with every employee, with repetition over time, as opposed to saying it one time only.

3. None of the tools should be too rigidly forced to be used on every single occasion. This avoids the "bureaucratic" theme that makes people feel force-fed and can foster feelings of resentment toward the tools and skills.

SUPPORTING RESEARCH FOR THIS CHAPTER

Baldwin, T. T., Ford, J. K., & Blume, B. D. (2009). Transfer of Training 1988-2008: An Updated Review and New Agenda for Future Research. In G.P. Hodgkinson and J.K. Ford (Eds.),

International Review of Industrial and Organizational Psychology (Vol. 24, pp. 41-71). Chichester, UK: Wiley.

Blume, B., Ford, J.K., Baldwin, T., & Huang, J. (2009). Transfer of training: A meta-analytic review. Journal of Management, 36, 1065-1105.

Burke, L.A. (2001). Training transfer: Ensuring training gets used on the job. In L.A. Burke (Ed.), High-impact training solutions: Top issues troubling trainers (pp. 89-116). Westport, CT: Quorum Books.

Burke, L. A., & Hutchins, H. M. (2007). Training transfer: An integrative literature review. Human Resource Development Review, 6, 263-296.

Colquitt, J. A., Lepine, J. A., & Noe, R. A. 2000. Toward and integrative of training motivation: A meta-analytic path analysis of 20 years of research. Journal of Applied Psychology, 85, 678-707.

Combs, J. G., Liu, Y., Hall, A. T., & Ketchen, D. J. 2006. How much do high performance work practices matter? A meta-analysis of their effects on organizational performance. Personnel Psychology, 59, 501-528.

Eisenberger, R., Stinglhamber, F., Vandenberghe, C., Sucharski, I.L., & Rhoades, L. (2002). Perceived supervisor support: Contributions to perceived organizational support and employee retention. Journal of Applied Psychology, 87, 565-573.

Facteau, J.D., Dobbins, G.H., Russell, J.E.A., Ladd, R.T., & Kudisch, J.D. (1995). The influence of general perceptions of the training environment on pretraining motivation and perceived training transfer. Journal of Management, 21, 1-25.

Ford, J.K., Quinones, M.A., Sego, D.J., & Sorra, J.S. (1992). Factors affecting the opportunity to perform trained tasks on the job. Personnel Psychology, 45, 511-527.

Goldstein, I., & Ford, J. K. 2002. Training in organizations (4th ed.). Belmont, CA: Wadsworth. Huczynski, A.A., & Lewis, J.W. (1980). An empirical study into the learning transfer process in management training. The Journal of Management Studies, 17, 227-240.

McSherry, M., & Taylor, P. (1994). Supervisory support for the transfer of team-building training.

The International Journal of Human Resource Management, 5, 107-119.

Paradise, A. (2007) ASTD State of the Industry Report, American Society of Training and Development, Alexandria, VA. Skinner, B.F. (1970). Walden Two. Macmillan, Toronto.

Smith-Jentsch, K.A., Salas, E. & Brannick, M.T. (2001). To transfer or not to transfer? Investigating the combined effects of trainee characteristics, team leader support, and team climate. Journal of Applied Psychology, 86, 279-292.

Tracey, J.B., Tannenbaum, S.I., & Kavanagh, M.J. (1995). Applying trained skills on the job: The importance of the work environment. Journal of Applied Psychology, 80, 239-252.

Tziner, A., Haccoun, R.R., & Kadish, A. (1991). Personal and situational characteristics influencing the effectiveness of transfer of training improvement strategies. Journal of Occupational Psychology, 64, 167-177

Chapter 5

Empowering Your CEMs With Authority, Resources, Information & Accountability

What Empowerment really is.

The clients we work with are often confused at first about what empowerment really means. No wonder – it gets used to mean motivation, inspiration, engagement and a host of other concepts. None of these is correct. Empowerment means enablement; giving employees everything they need to enable them to make good decisions and do good work. Employees who don't fully trust management's reaction to mistakes tend to true fear empowerment and actually prefer not to have it. Empowerment efforts often fail for this reason.

Earlier in this book we described the four things all customers want:

1. Accuracy and timeliness of information. Without CEM empowerment, information takes longer to obtain and to deliver to customers.

2. Ease and speed of doing business with you. Without CEM empowerment, the entire Event process takes longer – especially variance situations.

3. Choice/options. Without CEM empowerment, fewer choices are made available to customers because CEMs are unsure whether they have the authority to offer them.

4. Consistency. Without empowerment, decisions made by CEMs will vary, depending on individual personality traits such as boldness and self-direction. As a result, customers will experience inconsistent service experiences depending on which CEM they interact with. Customers find this inconsistency to be confusing and frustrating.

Withholding decision rights from customer service employees turns your organization into a sluggish, bureaucratic, inconsistent behemoth that frustrates customers. Today's customers want first-call resolution whenever possible. They want immediate access to decision makers. They want to entire Event process to be easy and painless. While this can't always be done, it can certainly be done more often.

Empowerment only occurs when employees are given adequate levels of all four of the following (A.R.I.A.):

1. Authority. CEMs are not empowered unless they are given decision rights: Gradually give employees more and more rights to make decisions. Don't do it all at once. This makes both managers and employees more comfortable, plus the inevitable mistakes that come with learning aren't as damaging. Make it crystal clear where their authority begins and ends. If this cannot be done, at least give them clear guidelines to use in decision-making. Assure them that if they follow the guidelines, they will be safe from harm even if they make a bad call.

These decision rights must be authentic – if you veto a decision you don't like, it sends a clear message that they don't own decision rights after all. If you don't agree with a decision someone makes, ask questions that teach the individual to think differently. *"I wonder how that decision might affect our profitability, what do you think?" "What else might work?"* Then allow them to come with a new decision themselves. This process is called coaching.

Authority is of particular importance for CEMs when you don't have a team-based model for applying metrics and measuring performance. Without a shared set of metrics that ties everyone together toward the same shared purpose, CEMs require all the more authority in order to get others to act on behalf of the customer's needs. Otherwise, you will not see the kind of improvements in Event service you are looking for.

Survey employees about authority in order to understand their perspectives on what authority they need in order to do their best work. *"Do you feel you have adequate authority to make things happen in order to meet customer commitments? What kinds of authority do you need ("Authority to make X department give me..." "Authority to get...information quickly" etc.)? For each answer, please explain what this authority will would allow you to achieve."*

2. Resources. CEMs are not empowered unless they are given all the resources that are essential to doing their jobs effectively. Resources can include access to data, budget for projects, adequate equipment and IT/software to easily gather and report customer issues and to enable Event team collaboration.

Survey employees about resources in order to understand their perspectives on what resources they need in order to do their best work. "Do you feel you are missing any resources that are essential to you doing your job (space, equipment, software, etc.)? For each answer, please explain the benefits you would expect."

3. Information. CEMs are not empowered unless they are given, and are given easy access to, all the information they need to make good decisions and do their work effectively. Information includes such things as customer data, skills training, repair status, warranty info, pricing and financial transparency.

Survey employees about information in order to understand their perspectives on what information they need in order to do their best work. *"What additional information do you need, which you do not presently have, that would make you more effective at your job (training, product inventory, issue status, current operational constraints, warranty info, pricing info, customer info, etc.)?"*

4. Accountability. CEMs are not empowered unless their performance is clearly tied to a sound performance management system that includes follow-up and feedback (coaching). The best form of accountability is self-accountability, when employees learn to hold themselves accountable to the highest standards.

Survey employees about accountability in order to understand their perspectives on what accountability they believe would be appropriate. *"Assuming these things are provided to enable you to execute your job more effectively, what kinds of responsibilities and outcomes do you believe you should be held accountable for in your role?"*

Create a proper balance between authority and accountability:

"Full-Input-Approval": For issues over which the employee has full authority they also have full accountability. For issues requiring management input there is mutual accountability between the employee and the manager. For issues requiring management approval the employee is not accountable since it is not his or her decision.

Final Thoughts

This book has been intentionally brief and concise to enable time-efficient reading. Nonetheless, it contains a great deal of important information that can potentially transform your business and delight customers like never before.

Now that you know what to do, you have the opportunity to do what you know. If you would like additional guidance in engineering the Customer Event Management function in your organization we invite you to contact us:

Brent.Finamore@thefinamoregroup.com.

Thank you for investing your time in this book.

Additional Books By Brent Finnamore

You can find these books on Amazon

Customer F.I.R.S.T.

Brent Finnamore brings you the ultimate formula of practical, proven, use-immediately tools and skills to manage customers and colleagues in any situation. It's all here - creating the right impression, mistake-proofing, handling upset customers, getting reliable commitments from colleagues, managing expectations, saying No without saying No, changing peoples' minds, gaining agreement, building trust, overcoming resistance and objections, creating innovative options for customers and getting more things done without working harder or longer. If you are a customer service professional, salesperson or manager, this book will be your daily guide to higher performance.

The 8-Step Professional Selling Process

Credibility, business savvy and political acumen form the prerequisites of top tier selling in today's complex business world. Brent Finnamore leverages his 25 years' experience in selling - and in training and coaching sales professionals and executives around the globe - to bring you the definitive 8-Step formula that cracks the code for winning large, premium-priced deals. Working with thousands of top producers, Brent has captured the very best sales practices, strategies and techniques and wove them together into one seamless, practical, reproducible methodology. The 8-Step PSP is essential reading for B2B sales professionals, managers and executives.

Achieving L.I.F.T.

Since 1992 Brent Finnamore has inspired and motivated more than 350,000 people across the globe, empowering them to harness their personal power and reach their business and career goals. Now for the first time, Brent distils his vast experience training tens of thousands of sales professionals to bring you The L.I.F.T. Formula and enable you to become a top producer in your field.

- Leverage your thoughts. How to think in ways that cause you to feel wonderful and empowered most of the time – even when things aren't going well.

- Ignite your wants. How to determine what you really want and intensify your desire for it by making it clear, detailed, action-oriented and aligned with your values.

- Forge deep belief. How to cultivate a feeling of certainty about your inherent ability to achieve what you want, about the excellent products and services you sell and about the great company you work for.

- Take regular action. How to get yourself to take consistent, routine action - and occasionally bold action - to move you toward your clear wants and goals

The Five Realizations for a Customer-Focused Organization

Customer-Focus is becoming a priority for more and more organizations and their competitors today for a good reason - a growing body of research is showing us that improving customer service is one of the highest return on capital investments a company can make. The 5 Realizations of a Customer-Focused Organization takes you through the five realizations and their corresponding criteria for a degree of customer-focus that delivers financial results.

The first Realization, *"If I get paid, I have customers,"* begins the transition to A Culture of Service.

The second Realization, *"We must do everything from the outside-in,"* paves the way to Customer Centricity.

The third Realization, *"We must not try to satisfy everyone, it's hard enough to delight some,"* leads to Focused Excellence.

The fourth Realization, *"We cannot know our customers too well,"* is the path to Customer Intimacy.

The fifth Realization, *"Everything starts and ends with leadership,"* begins a shift to Management Support.

Each of the five criteria are detailed and shown on a five-point scale for degree of realization, giving you a complete formula and a concrete action plan for implementation.

If you're ready to turn your organization's focus from inward to outward, the proven, concise methodologies found in this book by Brent Finnamore, founder of The Finnamore Group Inc. will show you the way.